Ultimate Profit Management

Over the course of the author's career as a banker and business consultant, he has seen many examples of businesses that were doing just "fine." They were profitable and growing slowly-but-surely, but then the business owner decided that it wasn't enough anymore to simply grow slowly. What was suddenly needed was growth of 20 percent, 50 percent, or even 100 percent per year, just like the notable companies they see and hear about every day in the media. They began to try to grow the business and, in a short period of time, a profitable and thriving business became unprofitable. Since the business was no longer profitable, it needed to take on debt in order to pay its expenses. After taking on more and more debt, the business reached a point where it was unable to find any more debt to take on. This circumstance caused the business to fail to pay its bills anymore, which led to a financial day of reckoning. It doesn't have to be this way. There is a more effective way to grow your business without causing it to become unprofitable. And that's why the author wrote this book. Growing a business without making profits usually leads to a short lifespan for that business and there are exceptions such as Uber and DoorDash—but, there is a big difference between a business that has outside investors (angel investors, private equity, and venture capital) and the typical small business entrepreneur trying to bootstrap a business. The difference is that if a business has a huge target market and it is growing its sales rapidly, outside investors may be willing to fund losses for a period. The same does not hold true for an entrepreneur trying to grow a business without outside investors. Losses show that a business is on borrowed time. Once your capital is exhausted, there is no going back. A business needs profits in order to remain viable and to be able to provide for its owners, its employees, and its community. Running a business that loses money will put you out of business. There is no reason to not be profitable as you grow your business! The author shares the lessons that were taught to him by leaders, mentors in business, and by his own clients. What took him by surprise was that these lessons aren't complicated. They're simple. They use simple, uncomplicated methods to grow their businesses profitably. You will learn about the readily available tools you can use to ensure that your business does not turn unprofitable as you grow it. You'll be convinced that it makes sense to resist the lure of the high-growth, no-profit strategy and instead embrace the approach of steady growth with profits. Use this book as a guide. In it, the author covers the most important aspects of reasonable, prudent growth that will avoid debt and allow you, your partners, and business associates a productive and non-stressful existence with a business that grows and profits correctly.

Ultimate Profit Management
Maximizing Profitability as You Grow Your Business

Manny Skevofilax

Routledge
Taylor & Francis Group

A PRODUCTIVITY PRESS BOOK

First published 2024
by Routledge
605 Third Avenue, New York, NY 10158

and by Routledge
4 Park Square, Milton Park, Abingdon, Oxon, OX14 4RN

Routledge is an imprint of the Taylor & Francis Group, an informa business

© 2024 Manny Skevofilax

ISBN: 978-1-032-71094-5 (hbk)
ISBN: 978-1-032-71097-6 (pbk)
ISBN: 978-1-032-71098-3 (ebk)

DOI: 10.4324/9781032710983

Typeset in Minion
by SPi Technologies India Pvt Ltd (Straive)

This book is dedicated to the memory of my mother and father, who immigrated to America from the island of Karpathos, and gave me the opportunity to pursue the American Dream.

Contents

About the Author

Manny Skevofilax is a consultant and speaker who helps business owners to make more money by successfully navigating the challenges of growing their businesses profitably. Since 2003, Manny has achieved extraordinary outcomes for his clients by using his experience in strategic planning, financial statement analysis, operations, organizational development, and team building.

A Baltimore, Maryland native, Manny earned a Bachelor of Science in Business and a Master of Science in Finance from the Merrick School of Business at The University of Baltimore.

Prior to starting his career as a consultant, Manny's background includes formal bank credit training and service as a Vice President with Comerica Bank, a US-based commercial lending institution. He has corporate lending experience in the United States and continental European markets, with specialties in commercial business finance, real estate finance, and large corporate syndicated lending for mergers and acquisitions.

Manny grew up in the restaurant business and made a career change to corporate banking at age 29. When he's not helping business owners, Manny can be found exploring the ancient ruins on the island of Karpathos where his parents were born.

Acknowledgments

Special thanks to you, Dr. Alan Weiss, for your encouragement. I am grateful for your mentorship. This book would not have been possible without you.

Introduction

Over the course of my career as a banker and business consultant, I have seen many examples of businesses that were doing just "fine." They were profitable and growing slowly, but surely. Then, one day, the business owner decided that it wasn't enough anymore to simply grow slowly. What was suddenly needed was growth of 20 percent, 50 percent, even 100 percent per year, just like the sexy companies they see and hear about every day in the media. They began to try to grow the business and, in a short period of time, a profitable and thriving business became unprofitable.

Since the business was no longer profitable, it needed to take on debt in order to pay its expenses. After taking on more and more debt, the business reached a point where it was unable to find any more debt available. This circumstance caused the business to fail to pay its bills anymore which led to a financial day of reckoning.

Have you ever heard a story like this before? Maybe not, because these sad stories are not popular and don't appear in the news too often. They are not exciting like the stories that talk about rapid growth! It doesn't have to be this way. There is a more effective way to grow your business without causing it to become unprofitable. And that's why I wrote this book.

Growing a business without making profits usually leads to a short lifespan for that business.[1] I know what you're going to say, "But, look at Uber, DoorDash, etc." You're correct! However, there is a big difference between a business that has outside investors (angel investors, private equity, venture capital, etc.) and the typical small business entrepreneur trying to bootstrap a business. The difference is that if a business has a huge target market and it is growing its sales rapidly, outside investors may be willing to fund losses for a period.

Often, even your outside investors come to a point where they don't want to invest in your business anymore.

The same does not hold true for an entrepreneur trying to grow a business without outside investors. Losses show that a business is on borrowed time. Once your capital is exhausted, there is no going back. A business needs profits in order to remain viable and to be able to provide for its owners, its employees, and its community. Running a business that loses money *will put you out of business*.

There is no reason to not be profitable as you grow your business! I will share with you the lessons that were taught to me by my teachers and mentors in business, and by my own clients. What took me by surprise was that these lessons aren't complicated. They're simple. They use simple, uncomplicated methods to grow their businesses profitably. You'll learn about the readily available tools you can use to ensure that your business does not turn unprofitable as you grow it. I hope you'll be convinced that it makes sense to resist the lure of the high-growth, no-profit strategy and instead embrace the approach of steady growth with profits.

Use this book as a guide. In it, I'll cover the most important aspects of reasonable, prudent growth that will avoid debt and allow you and your family a productive and non-stressful life, with a business that can enrich and reward future generations.

—**Manny Skevofilax**

NOTE

1 Only two-thirds of small businesses with employees survive after two years and about half survive at least five years: https://advocacy.sba.gov/wp-content/uploads/2023/03/Frequently-Asked-Questions-About-Small-Business-March-2023-508c.pdf.

1

Growth Philosophy

BOOTSTRAPPING ON YOUR OWN VS. FINDING INVESTORS

There are two primary ways to fund a business. The first is "bootstrapping," which means to fund the business yourself. The term bootstrapping originated with a phrase in use in the 18th and 19th centuries, "to pull oneself up by one's bootstraps." Back then, it referred to an impossible task. Today it refers more to the challenge of making something out of nothing. Still a formidable challenge. We're talking here about zero external investment. You begin by selling a product or service profitably. Your customers love your product or service and they love you!

Lest you think this is only for tiny businesses, Bill Hewlett and David Packard started the giant Hewlett-Packard in a garage in 1939 on their own dimes. When Fred Smith was trying to get Federal Express off the ground, it was widely circulated that he was able to meet an impending payroll in the nick of time via a successful night at poker.

Many of us who have begun our own professional services firms did so with no help financially because our start-up costs were minimal: a spare bedroom, some second hand office furniture, and an older computer. Ironically, as you'll see later in this book, financial problems can begin once success arrives: staffing up for higher volume, needing modern equipment, funding travel, and so forth. We'll get to that. But for now, beginning a business on a "shoestring budget" is quite possible and has plenty of precedent.

If you're good and disciplined (and somewhat lucky), you start selling more products and services profitably. Your business grows and you use your profits to fund it. You own 100 percent of your business. You're 100 percent in control of your business and you make all of the decisions.

DOI: 10.4324/9781032710983-1

All of this may sound ideal, but there are some *caveats* to consider:

- How much money can you invest, even with a highly conservative mindset?
- How do you handle unexpected events, such as a computer crash or the need for more professional calls for live and even remote meetings?
- What if family exigencies put pressure on the money you had allocated to bootstrap the business (illness, increase in rent, school costs, car breakdown)?

Thus, you ought to be clear on your total options, because even when bootstrapping seems to be a logical beginning, conditions can change. And, of course, many people don't even have the basic liquidity to fund their own businesses without endangering their other financial obligations.

FISCAL FINESSE

It makes no sense to be out on your own if you're also out in the street!

The second way is by finding investors to invest in your product or service. It gets a little complicated, so we'll keep it simple. For example, perhaps you have a great idea for a business, but you don't have enough money to start it. In this case, you can write a business plan and a "pitch deck" and try to convince outside investors to use their money to fund your idea.

Investors are going to want confirmation that your product/service has a place in its market, which is known as market validation. Thus, you're going to need "social proof" that your idea is pragmatic and immediately worthwhile. Remember that apps for smartphones took off immediately, but the Segway went nowhere (no pun intended). Social proof would make your case beyond your own promotion. For example, many financial and legal people specialize in managing estates and assets for widowed or divorced women, because these women previously didn't play any role in managing money. In many cases, they are uninformed about their actual holdings. It's easy to point to articles and studies that support that condition and the subsequent need.

Investors are going to need support and facts beyond your own enthusiasm. Don't be afraid of amounts, but be focused on your ability to convince and, ultimately, pay back the investors.

So the more the investment, the more the investors might want to be more closely and frequently involved in your progress. And that's entirely reasonable.

Investors are going to want a clearly defined return on their investment which they usually define in multiples (e.g., a return of at least ten times their investment). This has to be a "win/win" scenario, so that everyone feels well treated. You'll have to make some exceptions about transparency and difficulties, for example, to keep your financial partners trusting you, especially if you miss a deadline.

Investors are going to want a pre-defined exit timeframe. In other words, before they invest their money, they calculate when they plan to exit their investment in your company (usually 36 months). They are not intent on becoming your permanent partner, *they are intent often on investing in several firms like yours concurrently, seeking to make relatively short-term profits within a comfortable timeframe.*

Investors are generally going to want to play a role in the control of the business and its decision-making. They don't like surprises. They can accept setbacks if forewarned that might be the case, but not a promise unkept and surprising to them.

If you haven't already guessed, this is why family money—not yours, but relatives and even good friends—is never a great idea, because they have suddenly become investors with different sentiments and needs, rather than "just friends." Their expectations may be unrealistic, or you may have provided figures that were too optimistic.

In all candor, try not to borrow from family and don't pretend that it's a form of bootstrapping, because those aren't your boots any longer!

TWO SEPARATE BUSINESS MODELS

As you can imagine, the "convince investors" model can be quite difficult to achieve successfully. Entrepreneurs like you come up with new ideas every second. It can be challenging to convince an investor that your idea will be successful when your idea doesn't have any track record of market validation.

Here are some tips for accomplishing that.

- Point out that competition opens markets, it doesn't foreclose them. So something already in business resembling your product or service can substantiate (provide social proof of) the consumer/buyer's willingness to spend.
- Before seeking investors, offer free help or samples. Show that the product or service was well received, and ask your experimenters how much they would have paid for what they used.
- Create a marketing plan to prove how you'll achieve sales. Don't just include a source of buyers (e.g., alumni association, local community, and chamber of commerce) but also a *mechanism* for the sales (e.g., free Zoom session, complimentary webinar, and endorsement of an influential person).
- Gather several endorsements from people who are in key positions and will attest to the fact that your endeavor is appealing and marketable.
- Create a business plan that will show potential growth in revenues and expenses and, therefore, net margins over the next two years or so.

Potential investors can have wildly different definitions of market validation. One potential investor might think that 10,000 widgets sold in one year is satisfactory proof of market validation. Another potential investor might think that a million units sold in one year would be satisfactory.

Don't just tell, also ask. In other words, ask the investment sources what they consider reasonable goals to be. Make them jointly responsible for the financial expectations and timelines. And solicit sales ideas and help from them. We talked about a "mechanism" above. Some of your investors may have their own mechanisms which can lead to growth: peer meetings, club memberships, synergistic business investments, and so on.

It's imperative that you and your investors are "on the same side" and not engaged in adversarial positions. This is a "win/win" endeavor, not a zero-sum game where someone has to lose for someone else to win.

FISCAL FINESSE

This has to be "win/win." Choose investors with whom you can work best.

To achieve realistic and agreed-upon goals and timelines, investigate how other, successful startups achieved their current success. Did they begin during a certain season, with a physical presence, building on past contacts, and so forth?

Danger: What will usually undermine a new business with outside investors is the founder treating it as an extension of a hobby, and not a true business. When a woman we knew said she couldn't stay and chat because she had to get over to the new donut shop, we asked if the donuts were that good.

"I don't know" she said, "this will be my first time. But they're charging $6 for a donut, so I want to get there and try them before they're out of business next week."

Bootstrapping is the leading method of growing a business due to the difficulty in convincing investors to take a risk with an unproven business idea.

It's also the safest in terms of not being responsible to, and owing, outside interests whose return goals and timelines may be much harsher and less realistic than your own. Of course, not everyone has the wherewithal to fund their own startup business, but it's easier if you keep things simple and fairly small.

That includes your ego. Try not to engage assistants (virtual or real), office space, advertising, equipment, and so forth. That comes as a result of growth, but it doesn't stimulate early growth. I remember consulting with a startup owner who had a substantial staff. I noticed he had a hole in the back of his sweater, so I pointed it out.

A staff member said, "Oh, he knows. We call that 'an entrepreneur's sweater!'"

INVESTORS LOOK FOR SUPER-HIGH-GROWTH POTENTIAL AND CONTROLLING INTEREST

Instead of looking for slow and steady growth, investors are usually looking for ideas that have super-high-growth potential. Therefore, they are generally not interested in investing in a slow and steady growth business. (We'll discuss controlling the pace of growth in the next section.)

Investors (a) want their money and a profit returned, and (b) they want that as quickly as possible. Your business and marketing plans would have to demonstrate that those two objectives can be met reasonably. However, "reasonably" might mean two years of prudent risk to you and six months of hell-bent-for-leather risk-taking for the investors.

The greater the discordance, the greater the investors' need will be for control of the business. You have to be careful not to inadvertently become the investors' employee, and to maintain your position as founder and partner.

FISCAL FINESSE

The only thing worse than sweating blood for your own business is sweating blood for someone else's business interests.

That control can be subtle, expressed in polite memos and frequent Zoom calls, or it can be somewhat intimidating, with personal meetings that question why, where, when, and how you will accomplish certain goals.

Now, the reason that investors look for super-high-growth potential is that it is going to take a whole lot of sales and profits to enable them to make a 10× return on their investment in 36 months (which is the typical timeframe we cited earlier, although it may be shorter). If they've invested $1 million in your business, then they'll want $10 million returned to them.

That means profit, not revenues. In other words, *after* you pay the rent, equipment loans, salaries, insurance premiums, and so forth, you should have squirreled away enough to have $10 million available to repay your investors in three years. You can't expect this to magically show up at the end of three years. And you can't start saving only to draw down on it again if you have to pay bills beyond what the business is generating in profits.

That's why investors make reaching a certain "valuation" their biggest outcome when investing in a business. They will create an exit strategy which will include a challenging course for rapid revenue growth which, hopefully, will result in a valuation of $10 million at the end of three years.

Then, they plan to sell their stake to another investor. That is how they achieve a 10× return on their investment. It is simple, but it isn't easy!

Not only do founders with business partner investors face long hours and intervention about their progress, they also face doing much more with much less in their personal life. This obviously impacts the family in terms of less wealth as well as less time.

Given the above dynamics, keep in mind that when investors are proposing to invest money in your business, they typically want to have control of the decision-making in your business. In most cases, that translates into the investors owning at least 51 percent of your business. It's a reasonable condition from the investors' perspective, although you might not like the idea too much.

If you retained 51 percent (or better) ownership, you could overrule and ignore investors' demands for change. If it were 50/50, you'd have continual stalemate in disagreements. So it's only natural that an investor wants protection in the legal form of majority ownership. Very few will accept less (although family often will, which is why we've previously discouraged family investing).

In the worst case, you'll be outvoted. In the best case, you would have to influence, reason, and compromise when you're in disagreement. But you have that 36-month deadline looming out there, and it's an impetus for *inflexibility* on the part of investors. And guess what? The closer you approach it without being on schedule toward the 10× valuation, the more inflexible the investors will become.

FISCAL FINESSE

With investors, there is always a "payback" time and it's usually an immovable object.

This is not irresistible force meets immovable object. This is the founder running into a brick wall.

Investors are focused, they have a plan, and they've done the math. They have "been there and done that" with regard to making investments many times. This time might be your first time running a business. It is another reason that they seek to be in control.

We've talked about business and marketing plans to some degree. You'll have to convince the investors that you're a mature business person, even if you haven't begun a business before. You can do this by:

- Having realistic revenue and profit goals (little at the outset, growing after the first year);
- Being careful not to be profligate: investing in a large office, administrative people, and so forth;
- Being careful about hires; don't use family members on salary unless they have clear and vital expertise;
- Not hesitating to work a long day and an occasional weekend, including meeting with the investors.

You don't have to have started prior businesses to be perceived as a level-headed business person. You do have to make concessions and compromises with your investor partners. You can't be fighting them like a salmon swimming upstream. Salmon die after that upstream swim.

Maybe that "immovable object" can be budged a bit if you're perceived as someone who is trying the best at all times.

CONTROLLING THE PACE OF GROWTH

As promised, we'll now turn to controlling the pace of growth. When you choose the bootstrapping method to fund the growth of your business, you control the pace of growth in your business. This is important because with proper planning and monitoring, you can ensure that your business stays profitable and thriving.

Growth is essential, so the choice is never "no growth." But the speed and volume of the growth will be dictated by your product or service, your market, your available investment finances, *and your temperament*. You can see a part of these relationships in Figure 1.1.

Thus, if you're willing to take substantial risk but generate low growth, you're making poor choices. If you'll only tolerate low (or no) risk and you generate low growth, you'll inevitably fail. High growth fueled by high risk will generate a very aggressive success, but the question is, for how long? However, if you can generate significant growth with low risk, you've found

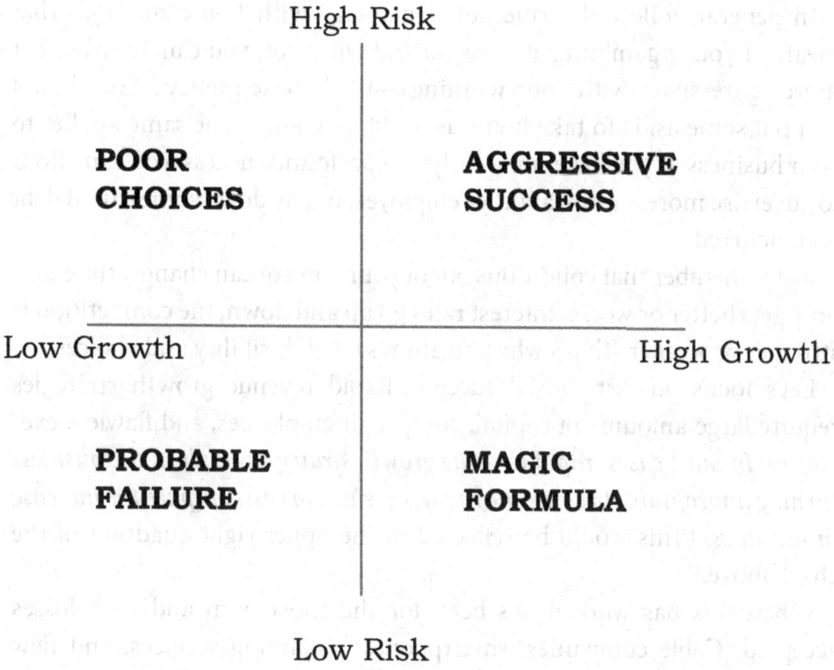

High Risk

POOR CHOICES	**AGGRESSIVE SUCCESS**

Low Growth ——————————————— High Growth

PROBABLE FAILURE	**MAGIC FORMULA**

Low Risk

FIGURE 1.1
Risk and growth opportunities.

the "magic formula." (Many services come to market with low investment and low risk and can do quite well. Think of service warranties—that are seldom used—or virtual assistants.)

You can still choose to follow an aggressive growth strategy—the choice is yours. The best strategy to follow is to always put yourself in a position where you have choices, you can make changes rather quickly, and, most of all, you're comfortable. Some people enjoy "bluffing" at poker in order to win a big hand even if they don't have very powerful cards. That's a decent strategy for those with nerves of steel, but not so much for those who begin to perspire and twitch!

FISCAL FINESSE

There are differences between "prudent risk" and "excessive risk." But in business, there's no such thing as "no risk."

In general, follow the rule about playing "with house money." That means if you're gambling at a casino and win a lot, you can afford to bet more aggressively with your winnings—the "house money." You should still put some aside to take home as profit, of course. The same applies to your business. If you have some early and profound success, you can afford to advertise more, or hire another employee, or pay down some initial debt you incurred.

Just remember that conditions out of your control can change: the economy gets better or worse, interest rates go up and down, the competition is stronger or weaker. That's why you always need flexibility and choices.

Let's focus on fast, initial success. Rapid revenue growth strategies require large amounts of capital, competent employees, and flawless execution. *In most cases, rapid revenue growth strategies result in the business turning unprofitable because the rapid increases in costs outpace the increase in revenues.* (This would be reflected in the upper right quadrant of the chart above.)

When this has worked, it's been for the short term and with losses accepted. Cable companies, smartphones, streaming services, and new investment services have often taken early losses, driving the competition out of the market, and then raising prices when they are one of the few (or only) alternatives left standing.

You may not have the financing (or the courage) to watch losses mount as your customers and orders grow. But it is a legitimate option if you have the nerve and the potential *to dominate your market.* The infomercials you see on TV cost millions to produce, but the business owners are counting on a huge payoff from the publicity. (Which is why they're often on at midnight or later when rates are cheaper!)

The point, obviously, is that the light at the end of this tunnel can't be an approaching train. You have to be confident that you can reach a point where the growth and publicity will enable you to raise prices, "upsell" the current products and services, and/or dramatically lower these investments. Once you're successful, well, you don't see Rolls-Royce or Bentley having to advertise on TV.

Let's look at the opposite. If your business turns unprofitable, it will start costing you cash to run it. Therefore, it's important to have enough cash on hand to weather the period of unprofitability (and, if you're using investors, to either provide them with some payments or demonstrate you don't need more of *their* money).

How long will this period of unprofitability last? Only you can estimate the answer to this question, based on your internal projections and your actual financial results. If you don't have enough cash to get through this period, you place the whole business at risk of failure.

You don't need profit *immediately*, but you need it eventually; not "someday." All businesses can run into cash flow challenges. The remedy is to expect (or even predict) them and have a plan for pulling out of the tailspin. That can include more investment funds available, a shift to less expensive but still-effective marketing, forestalling planned investments (especially in non-marketing activities), and acquiring expert outside help.

It's not unusual to be so caught up in the process that you lose sight of your goals while you redouble your efforts! That's the "hamster phenomenon." A good business advisor can help you in the short term determine whether you're approaching your goal or just running in circles. Remember that a business can succeed forever, but it only gets to fail once.

IN LIGHT OF THE ABOVE, WE'LL FOCUS ON THE BOOTSTRAPPING METHOD

Now you have a good idea of how the two ways work to fund the growth of your business. Both methods have their own set of unique challenges. This book will focus on the bootstrapping method of growing your business.

That's because our experience is overwhelmingly that this is the most likely method to produce success with minimum risks.

- You're not dealing with the vagaries of outside investors who have their own set of objectives and expectations.
- You're in charge. The defeats are yours and so are the victories. Plus you don't have the opportunity to blame others and not take accountability.
- The financial burdens are less, even though you have to generate your own money because you're not under pressure to produce a 10× return over the first three years.
- Frankly, it's more fun. And when you're having fun, you're more committed, passionate, and positive. You'll stay healthier.

You've "bootstrapped" other things, after all, such as painting the house, or refurbishing a car, organizing a fund-raiser, and so forth. Look back on those successes to remind you that you're quite capable of creating impressive results on your own.

Passion, as just mentioned, plays a large role in the success of bootstrapping. If you're passionate about your mission, the massive effort required to find success will not feel like "work."

People generally awake with one of two temperaments.

- Wow, another day, I have bills to pay, calls I don't want to make, problems to solve, and follow-ups with people who are late. It's another long, slow crawl through enemy territory.
- Wow, another day. I can't wait to inform everyone I can of the value I can bring to them. This will be a great day.

The first attitude is one of "taking," in that you're trying to build a business to make money ("take money from people"). The second is one of "giving," in that you're trying to provide value to people.

If you feel as if you're "taking" you'll be reluctant to reach out to prospects because you think they'll see you as interrupting them. But if you feel you're "giving" then you won't hesitate to reach out because *you're trying to help people.*

These are attitudes, not capital investments! If you're passionate about helping people, then you'll be far more comfortable enthusiastically reaching out to them. And remember that enthusiasm is contagious.

And this is why you can never really expect someone else to market your business as well as you do. They will never have your passion!

Perseverance will also play a large role in your success. You'll face constant challenges and obstacles in your path to success. That's just part of life and business. Just when you feel like you have a good handle on your business, something inevitably will fly in out of nowhere and throw a wrench in your well-laid plans. (We call this the "seagull effect.")

A great example is the saga of the impact of COVID-19 on small businesses. Who could have reasonably predicted that? You must be willing to persevere, again and again, in order to get where you want to go in your business. And which businesses did best during COVID-19? Those with money on hand!

FISCAL FINESSE

Resilience is the most important trait of business owners. It's not that they never fail, it's that when they fail, they "fail forward."

Your finances *and your attitude* have to provide you with the perseverance to overcome setbacks and realize that success is the ultimate result of bouncing back from many setbacks. Isolate your setbacks: This happened today with this person under these conditions. It doesn't mean that my products won't be seen positively by others. And generalize your victories: This happened today not because I'm lucky or this person happened to like me, but because I have a great product!

The information that I am going to share in this book applies to businesses that have no formal outside investors such as venture capital or private equity.

This book is dedicated to the entrepreneurs that are in the arena every day, independently fighting—and thinking—their way to success.

2

Staffing: Before, During, or After

IF YOU BUILD IT, THEY MIGHT NOT COME!

Hiring during the growth phase can be tricky and that requires caution. It's a great example of the chicken and the egg conundrum! Do you hire the new employees in anticipation of new sales or as the sales start to materialize? It's a delicate balancing act that is influenced by the amount of your business's profitability.

The famous *Field of Dreams* statement, "Build it and they will come," is missing a line in terms of marketing, including attracting employees:

Build it
Tell them you've built it
And they will come

The questions about staffing are twofold for a new business: *When* do you hire, and *whom* do you hire?

We recommend that you do not staff-up ahead of time, no matter how rosy prospects may appear. Once you're stuck with overhead (payroll, insurance, taxes, benefits, absenteeism, and so forth), it's hard to get rid of all of it. People can sue for illegal dismissal, contract violations, and even invent the cause. This entails legal expenses, as well as possible stains on your brand and reputation.

But your business will require new employees to handle increased sales. Let's say you're generating $5 million in sales right now and plan to add $500,000 in sales this year. You could hire the new employees right

DOI: 10.4324/9781032710983-2

now, but what happens if the sales don't show up? That's our example, above.

FISCAL FINESSE

It's harder to find new sales than it is to find new employees, so focus on the former before the latter.

We suggest that you begin to hire *when new business is consummated*, not when you "feel good about it" or are even "promised" it. A prospect can "undo" a promised piece of business, but you can't so easily "undo" a new hire.

This is why it's equally important to consider *whom* to hire.

My mentor, Alan Weiss, believes in "the 1% solution®" which means that if you improve by one percent a day, in 70 days you're twice as good! (You can do the math on your calculator if you're skeptical.) The following may be your one percent:

> You can rather easily teach people the content of your business and teach them practices and procedures. But you can't teach enthusiasm, energy, and discipline. These are innate traits. So look for and hire those with the latter, don't focus on "X years of experience in the industry." These days, that's irrelevant, and it's often simply one year repeated five or ten times.

Thus, hire people who can "hit the ground running" with energy and enthusiasm for your business. You can teach them almost anything else you need.

You have made a significant investment in employees, benefits, computers, cell phones, office space, and related overhead. But your business is now unprofitable. What choices do you have?

The first order of business is to remain positive. You can't fix a problem *until you know its cause*. What is the cause for less profit than you had predicted?

- Overzealous plan
- Delayed buying decisions by legitimate prospects
- Events out of your control
  - Economic shift
  - New technology
  - New competition
- Higher than expected expenses

Don't immediately "dump" money into the business. Instead, try to figure out why you're behind plan. That really shouldn't take more than a couple of hours of honest thinking and a few discussions with people you trust.

Believe it or not, that challenge occurs more than you think, due to the human spirit of enthusiasm and positive mental attitude. We don't like to talk about potentially missing our goals. We certainly don't want to be considered naysayers. Therefore, I counsel my clients to say that they are being "prudent" about their hiring practices.

To tie together the major points of this segment, deviations from business plans are most often caused by poor hiring. "Poor" hiring means people hired too soon, before new business is closed; hiring the wrong people (especially family because you think they'll be inexpensive and very devoted); and paying too much for people.

This is why we're stressing that it's easier to find people than it is new business, and the people whom you hire have to come to the party with significant abilities that can't be "taught" such as energy and enthusiasm.

We too often allow our egos to generate hiring, as though subordinates are a sign of success and power, and "assistants" (virtual or real) demonstrate how busy you are. In reality, we know a great many solo entrepreneurs who are quite happy subcontracting for help when they need it and otherwise merrily getting along without any permanent staff, while they make well into seven figures every year.

HIRE SLOWLY AND MAINTAIN FOCUS ON PROFITABILITY

For example, let's say you want to grow your revenues quickly by hiring three new salespeople. However, your financial situation is such that you will require an immediate financial contribution from the salespeople in order to be able to make their payroll.

What are the probabilities?

- **You hire dynamos who absolutely hit the ground running and produce a ton of new business**. What are the odds of that? *Very low.* Why? Because these people are already doing well elsewhere and making a lot of money. You'd have to provide very handsome packages for them to move. That will decrease your margins. And not everyone can sell everything immediately. They would need some acclimation time.
- **You hire people who aren't currently all-stars but you're willing to invest in their training and development**. The odds of them succeeding? Moderate, but at some cost. You'll have to take the time to train them, or assign someone else to train them, which will hurt your margins. Then they'll need some "ramp-up" time as they hit the phones or the road and begin to sell or service.
- **You wait, perhaps working harder yourself (and asking any current employees to work harder)**. Even if you're paying overtime or bonuses for the extra effort, the probability is that you'll develop and sustain new business until that profitability allows you to more easily hire the all-stars or to take the time to develop the non-all-stars.

FISCAL FINESSE

You're better off working harder for new business and then bringing on more staff to handle it, than bringing on staff in advance and working harder to support the staff.

The first situation will most likely fail because a new salesperson requires a lead time in order to get up and running, and close sales. *One rule of thumb is that a new salesperson requires a minimum of three months to start producing sales.* Even that "all-star" will require that "ramp-up" time to some degree. Plan to have at least three months of their payroll in your bank account before you hire that salesperson. If you hire two, you're talking six months—three months for each.

Ask yourself: What portion of my business's profits am I able to commit to hiring new employees? Focus on hiring people as your profitability permits it and make sure you take into consideration the full cost of each hire.

You don't want to hire people by going into debt. That's not a profitable, growing business. So if you can't afford someone (think about the three-month rule above), then don't hire them!

At the outset, you have several choices with profits. These choices will multiply as your business grows and profitability continues to increase. But for now, with a newer business, consider this: Revenues must exceed expenses a short time after startup. You can't afford to run a business in the "red" for a long period. Many people attempt this by going through their retirement plans, college savings for children, and maximizing credit card debt. They will even borrow from family members.

But if you continue to run your business with expenses exceeding revenues, there's a word for it: bankruptcy.

Simply put, your revenue has to cover the following.

- Business operating expenses: Your salary, others' salaries, office rental or mortgage, infrastructure costs (furniture, equipment, and machinery), insurance, retirement plans, repairs, maintenance, taxes, and so forth.
- Your salary has to cover your family and/or personal expenses: rent or mortgage, retirement savings,[1] insurance, household expenses, school payments, and so forth.
- You'll need a contingency ("rainy day") fund for business and personal needs that may arise: accidents, repairs, replacements, helping relatives, breakdowns, and related unplanned but important needs.

You can't think about hiring anyone not already on your staff unless these needs are being covered by revenues. If you hire someone and then have to let them go, you've lost a *lot* of money in making that mistake.

THE FULL COST OF A HIRE IS LIKE AN ICEBERG: MOST IS BELOW THE SURFACE

Be sure to take into consideration the full cost of your new hire. It's not just the salary alone that you need to consider. There are, for example, payroll taxes that sometimes don't get factored into your initial analysis.

Payroll taxes consist of the employer's Social Security match (FICA), Federal Unemployment Tax (FUTA), and State Unemployment Tax (SUTA).

This is a good time to mention that you're going to need a good accountant—not your cousin Elaine or someone working out of a bedroom. Ideally, a small agency with a few people (like you, not much overhead to have to cover) *which is well-versed in small businesses, especially newer ones.* These people can tell you what you need and don't need.

FISCAL FINESSE

Don't attempt to use software for your monthly books, reconciliation, general ledger, taxes, and so forth, if you have never done it before. Do you try to fix the brakes on your car yourself when it's not stopping quickly enough?

A good accountant (firm) will do your monthly financials and reconciliations, including your check book for under $1,500 per month, depending on your type of business and needs.

There is also the cost of your business's Workers Compensation Insurance policy. Don't forget about the costs of your business's employee benefits like health insurance, vision insurance, and dental insurance. Factor in annual raises and bonuses, too.

And this is the point to remind you that you need an attorney equivalent to your accountant. A small firm specializing in other small firms. Ideally, your attorney should be very responsive and be able to handle:

• Trademarks	• Employee contracts
• Infringements	• Local, state, and federal filings
• Litigation threats	• Employee problems

In the early growth phase of your business, you do not need a "human resources" function, either real or virtual. And you don't want an attorney who did your house closing or your will. Between the accountant and the attorney, they should be able to handle all aspects of your incorporation and continuing compliance with applicable laws. This is a litigious society, so passing things by these people *in advance* is always smart.

In order to keep it simple, I advise my clients to take the expected annual salary and add 15 percent to that number to account for payroll taxes. Then, add an annual cost for employee benefits, raises, and bonuses. For example, if the annual salary is $100,000, then add $15,000 (15 percent) for the payroll taxes. Then, start to make some assumptions based on your current costs.

For example, add $12,000 for a single person's health benefits, $3,000 (3 percent for a cost-of-living raise) and $10,000 for an annual bonus. Let's add those numbers together and we get $140,000. That number is 40 percent higher than the employee's annual salary!

You can see why recklessly and haphazardly adding employees *before the benefits of growth are realized* can be very expensive!

We still didn't account for the cost of the computer, desk, chair, and office space. Once you account for those costs, you're approaching a number that is 50 percent higher than the salary you started with.

Therefore, hire slowly, focus on profitability, and make sure that you're getting the "bang for your buck" with each and every employee.

HOW TO GET FIVE HATS ON ONE HEAD

As the CEO of a growing business, you'll wear most of the hats for a long time. As the owner of a business that has chosen the bootstrapping method of growth, it's important to mentally prepare yourself to the fact that you'll still play the most important role in your business for a long time.

Most people who complain of "horrible bosses" and "burdensome conditions" in business don't understand that the founder of a business will be working harder and longer than any employee of any business, large or small. That's why whining does not help and complaining only hurts. But for those of you who are or will be refugees from larger businesses, you can manage your time well.

The "hats" you'll be wearing are those that include founder and owner, CEO, financial expert, operations expert, marketer, sales professional, repair person, and so forth. How can you handle all this, how can you keep up your spirits, and be a role model to others?

There is an old canard in the speaking profession that someone comes upon a mason and asks, "What are you doing?" The mason replies, "I'm laying bricks." The person moves on to a second mason who is asked the same question. That mason replies, "I'm building a cathedral." The story ends there and is supposed to demonstrate the difference between a job and a career.

Alan Weiss has taught me another way to look at this. There's a third mason, and when asked what that mason is doing, the mason replied, "I'm bringing people closer to God."

That, my friends, is a "calling," and that's the secret of wearing a lot of hats and wearing them well.

FISCAL FINESSE

When you start your own firm be careful not to end up with a worse boss than you had at the large company you left!

Yes, you will have key employees that are loyal and dependable and treat your business like it's their business. If you're a good person to work with, these folks will stick with you.

Family employees sometimes work out. But, too often, they don't. That's because:

- It's hard to have a different relationship on the job from the one at home;
- If remote work is involved, you'll find them more distracted and you'll be even more concerned about "getting your money's worth";
- Their knowledge of you and the family history and traditions can undermine the working hierarchy;
- By non-family employees, they will be considered "insiders" and "favored";
- It's easy for them to take advantage, to take excess time off, to use company equipment and supplies, and even to expose you to legal difficulties.

Hence, we advise against family employees. There are exceptions, of course, and many founders have left their businesses to their children. However, there's an old saying that has the germ of truth in it: First generation founds the business, second generation expands the business, and third generation ruins the business.

The "calling" isn't always passed down or shared.

Although you will be surrounded by some great people, you'll find that you're still the "chief" in many roles in your business. In my experience, many bootstrappers get frustrated that they can't simply delegate away all of the difficult responsibilities in their business and only work on the easy stuff. In fact, you'll find that it is quite the opposite!

(And to speak to a specific group, we've found that former military officers who retire and set up their own business, but are accustomed to having a great many subordinates as resources, suffer from this more than most.)

You *can* delegate to subcontractors, to the client, and to professional firms (e.g., accountants, lawyers, designers, technologists). But don't try to delegate to family not involved in the business. (Have you ever heard a partner say, "You know, you're not at work now!") And be careful about "virtual" anything. We discussed earlier that virtual assistants are mainly for ego at this point, but some people will urge you to go on websites and use people in Asia for various tasks, from web design to eliciting leads. Don't do this, because you'll wind up spending more time with them than you would doing it yourself *and* you'll be spending money, no matter how "economical." I can't tell you how many entrepreneurial clients we've had who hired foreign technology "expertise" who later had to abandon the entire project.

For starters, you will be your business's Chief Executive Officer: responsible for all decisions. What does that entail?

Here's what a CEO traditionally does: Manages and directs the company toward its primary goals and objectives. Oversees employment decisions at the executive level of the company. Leads a team of executives to consider major decisions, including acquisitions, mergers, joint ventures, or large-scale expansion.

In your case, your desk is where the buck stops, to quote former President Truman. If your employees don't do something correctly or overlook something, there's someone else who can back them up or correct them, perhaps even you. But if *you* don't do things correctly or forget something, there is no backup. For example, if you're so busy fighting fires that you can't spend time on strategy, *then no one else is either, and you won't have a strategy!*

FISCAL FINESSE

Are you working ON the business or IN the business? It had better be the former.

"CEO" is a nice title, but it implies some very important work and "heavy lifting." It's not fulfilled by what's printed on your business card or listed on your website, but rather by how you behave every day.

Most of all, you're a role model for others' behavior.

You'll find that you're still your business's Chief Sales Officer (CSO) and responsible for a large portion of its sales.

This is one circumstance where you can't avoid being the lead salesperson. We've talked about a "calling" and the need for energy and enthusiasm. If you can't sell your products or services, how can you expect anyone else to do so? And you are also the main role model for sales.

No one believes what they read or hear in organizations. They only believe what they *see.* No matter how customer-oriented you claim to be, if you eschew talking to customers and prospects, your people will assume it's not all that important for them, either.

What does a CSO or a Chief Revenue Officer (CRO) do? A CSO (often called a CRO today) is responsible for ensuring the team achieves targeted growth and meets sales revenue targets. The CSO is at the top of the sales hierarchy and frequently oversees sales vice presidents and sales managers. Those supervisors, in turn, oversee the salespeople who make up the bulk of the team.

We know what you're thinking: I don't have a sales hierarchy, or sales officers, or the "bulk of a team"! No new business owner does, normally. Hence, you have to fill a multiplicity of sales roles, including prospecting, lead generation, sales meetings, proposal writing, closing, and account management.

Since you'll be starting with just a few clients in all probability, you can certainly handle this. If you have too many clients to handle, that's a good problem and means you can do some of that hiring we suggested, once business is confirmed and in the door!

You'll still be the Chief Financial Officer, responsible for the financial decisions. Chief Financial Officers (CFOs) hold the top financial position in an organization. They are responsible for tracking cash flow and financial planning, analyzing the company's financial strengths and weaknesses, and proposing strategic directions.

This may be a strength or weakness of yours (very few people are excellent at wearing all these "hats"), but you have access to your outside resources: accounting team, advisors, bankers, and so forth. You should rely on them for support and advice.

Don't try to negotiate major financing or debt consolidation on your own. For that matter, don't even use software for your monthly books or tax reporting. Here's the key: If your expertise were in supply chain improvement, for example, would you advise a client to try to attack that issue alone, or would you advise using an expert, like yourself? Well, the same principle applies to you. We've seen financial messes that have resulted from do-it-yourself financial attempts, web software, and others' endorsements of shortcuts.

As CFO, don't risk messing up your business's books or the inability to improve your credit by taking shortcuts and trying to save a few bucks. There is a Chinese proverb about trying to economize that goes something like this: *The price of using candles in the dark is twins.*

You will find that these responsibilities require your leadership. Leadership is the ability of an individual or a group of people to influence and guide followers or members of an organization, society, or team. Leadership often is an attribute tied to a person's title, seniority, or ranking in a hierarchy.

You can try to lead because of your business card or status: CEO, president, founder, and so on. You can lead by using "carrots and sticks," reward, and punishment. You can lead through your expertise because you know more than anyone else. *Or you can lead through respect: We call this "referent leadership."* People follow you because they trust and respect you and know you have their best interests in mind, not merely your own.[2]

If you recall, we pointed out that no one in organizations believes what they read or hear, only what they *see*. Hence, the leader's actions—your actions—will create the culture that governs organizational behavior.

FISCAL FINESSE

Alan Weiss says: *Culture is merely that set of beliefs which govern behavior.*

As you'll see in Figure 2.1, beliefs create attitudes which are manifest in behaviors. What beliefs are you manifesting for people to emulate?

As your business grows and you improve your financial position, hiring will become easier. If you already have employees, they will become "ambassadors" to new talent and hires because they enjoy working for you.

Beliefs

Attitudes

Behaviors

FIGURE 2.1
From beliefs to behavior. From Fearless Leadership, Alan Weiss, Routledge, 2020.

If your new hires will be your first employees, they will have learned of you through your success and word-of-mouth.

That's the good news! But your time will become more stretched as you take on more managerial responsibilities and more "human resources" focus (benefits, reference checking, salary negotiations, vacations, employment contracts, and so on).

Don't bite off more than you can chew, because it will hurt your work/life balance. You don't want to wear these hats on top of each other nor do you want to change them every ten minutes. You need to find your "flow" and your comfort zone. Many of these areas overlap (e.g., building sales and hiring salespeople).

There are two underlying dynamics that can "make or break" any new business. One is monetary and the other is relationships. They are obviously inextricably entwined. Keep your eye on the financial ball, but also make your family and/or personal interests a high priority. They will add to your sense of well-being or create a doom-loop if you're not careful.

Finally, there is a reason I included a chapter about technology (Chapter 8) in this book. In my experience, many business owners are not using apps and software to help them become better organized and more efficient. Since you'll be wearing multiple hats for years, do yourself a favor and spend some time to learn about these tools.

They will change your life.

NOTES

1 Business retirement can be in the form of a Simplified Employee Pension individual retirement account (SEP IRA) or 401k pension plan or other qualified retirement benefit. Personal retirement includes regular IRAs, Roth IRAs, and so forth.

2 For an excellent exploration of leadership, read John W. Gardner on Leadership, Free Press, 1989. Yes, it's an older work, but it's still superb.

3

Avoiding the Eight Growth Mistakes

SETTING UNREASONABLE GROWTH GOALS

Every entrepreneur has a personal opinion of reasonable growth goals for the business that's been created. But is there a metric that will provide some confidence and assurance that such growth goals are reasonable?

One reality is that the metric for someone else isn't necessarily the one for you. There's a psychological dynamic called "projection," which means that we project our own strengths and weaknesses onto others (even with the best of intentions). Hence, if I couldn't ski well enough on my first outing to manage the intermediate hills, I assume you won't be able to, either, and I'm comfortable telling you that!

The trouble is, if I trust you, I'm inclined to accept your opinion, which may lead to underperformance on my part—because I may be a naturally adept skier. Conversely, if you tell me to expect at least 70 percent growth in the first three years (because you did) and I only achieve 50 percent, I may feel like a failure.

Consequently, we have to arrive at our own, relevant, reasonable growth goals.

So, where do we look? We can examine these options:

- Average startup growth overall
- Average startup growth for our business
- Coaches and consultants who specialize in such ventures and/or on markets
- The current economy and competitive environment.

The reason that it's important to take time to consider "due diligence" in setting growth goals is that the wrong ones can place both short-term and long-term tremendous burdens on your nascent business. You might well

DOI: 10.4324/9781032710983-3

have the financial resources to pursue unreasonable growth goals. But you may run out of cash in that crazed pursuit. There's a technical term for spending more than you're taking in over long periods: bankruptcy.

Unreasonable growth places an unreasonable burden on your business. One issue is the chicken/egg, build/buy quandary: Do you staff-up to meet elevated growth goals, or do you wait for the business and, if successful, run the risk of not being able to implement and fulfill because you're scrambling to find staff with the right skills? (This, obviously, is a more chronic problem post-pandemic than ever before.)

You and your people can burn out from overwork and become highly stressed as goals remain on the distant horizon and lose the credibility and faith of lenders, supporters, existing customers, and family.

FISCAL FINESSE

If you're losing money on every transaction, you can't make it up with volume.

I hope you're beginning to realize that prudent risk is fine, but excessive risk—even from supreme confidence—can land you in a morass of debt. And this is like quicksand: The harder you struggle, the more you sink.

To become proficient in any pursuit usually requires repetition, whether it's ice skating, guitar playing, Angry Birds®—or business growth. But this last goal seems to be a paradox: How do you achieve growth if you have no practice doing so?

Yet we all have some experience improving and increasing things in at least small but important ways. That's why *reasonable* growth is so critical to our thinking. We may, at any given point in our business evolution, not have certain key elements in place to sustain rapid growth:

• Infrastructure	• Financing
• Brand recognition	• Staff
• Customer referrals	• Skills and talent
• Technological edge	• Technology
• Variety of offerings	• Time

Growth requires repetition of existing habits and the application of existing skills to begin progress to exploit what you already have and to acquire what you need. Your family isn't always the best source for this help. I advocate going outside your own environment because "when you have your face pressed up against the glass, you can't see the big picture." This might mean forming a knowledgeable advisory board, joining trade and professional associations, attending workshops and seminars (in person or remotely), and doing some extensive reading.

Let's simplify this by applying what I call the "SIR System," which stands for "Sustain, Improve, Replace."[1] You can see this in Figure 3.1.

Ask yourself and your advisors and family:

- What has sustained us to this point that clearly will also *sustain* us to reasonable growth?
- What has sustained us to this point but must be *improved* if we are to attain reasonable growth?
- What has caused us problems and been inadequate to this point that we cannot improve but must instead *replace*?

Let's move ahead now to learn how to avoid the siren call of unreasonable growth.

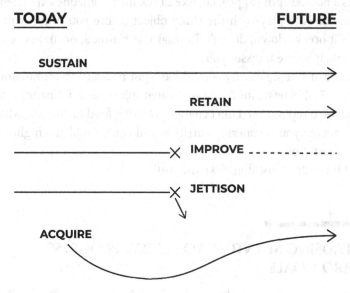

FIGURE 3.1
The "SIR System."

SHINY NEW TOY SYNDROME IMPEDES YOUR FOCUS

I once worked for a corporation where everyone was in terror when the boss went to a workshop or seminar because she would come back with the latest "new idea" and want to change everything that was in place. This happened so often that productivity plummeted during all the reorganizations.

Stores put "shiny objects" at the end of aisles and at checkout registers, so as to gain attention and secure impulse purchases. And today's shiny toy becomes yesterday's shiny toy when a new shiny toy comes along tomorrow.

FISCAL FINESSE

If you think every shiny object is a trend, just think about "pet rocks" and the "hula hoop." When is the last time you saw one?

In business, the result is a shift away from your goal and toward what appears to be something better. This causes "short-term goal hopping" and results in the unconscious abandonment of longer-term, strategic goals. (Popularly, this is termed "FOMO"—fear of missing out. I used to think this was a bookkeeping approach, like LIFO, until someone explained it.)

My advice is to play with the shiny object before you implement anything. If it breaks down, doesn't do what was claimed, or makes your life worse, toss it before it tosses you.

Someone at Boeing clearly should have put pilots in the simulators for the new 737 Max jets. Not doing so created injury, death, financial chaos, and a harmed reputation. Don't change your dog food formula to what the researchers tell you is superior nutrition and can be sold at a higher price until you test it out.

What if the dogs just don't like the stuff?

NOT PAUSING MONTHLY TO REVIEW PROGRESS TOWARD GOALS

Reviewing progress quarterly (or even less often) is woefully insufficient. Do you check your car's gas tank monthly or wait to pay your mortgage quarterly? You'd run out of gas and out of credit.

There's no sense having goals unless you have metrics: measurements of progress toward your goals.

And why don't business owners review their progress more often? Wait for it…because they're too busy! But busy doing what? What's so important that it takes precedence over monitoring performance against expectations?

FISCAL FINESSE

After you unlock the door and turn on the lights in the morning, the next job is to monitor current performance against plans. Yes, with coffee.

On a monthly basis, you'll get a good idea of business performance. But a quick review weekly (or even daily) is the best way to avoid surprises.

- The Figbee payment hasn't arrived and it's late.
- The new software was supposed to be online this week and it isn't.
- Our margins are down by 1 percent without any clear reason.

You can identify negative trends before they do great damage and exploit positives before they disappear. You can track expenditures as they are actually processed and reported. You can find out if you're on, over, or under budget. You can compare the current status to last month's and last year's, and your projection.

All of this provides peace of mind and the ability to actively work on the business and not merely in the business.

HIRING (AND KEEPING) THE WRONG PEOPLE FOR THE JOB

If the pandemic and its aftermath have taught us anything, with "quietly quitting" and "great resignations," it's that simplistically merely seeking and replacing "bodies" is woefully insufficient. You must consider what your *future* needs are, not merely replace people dealing with the old ones. In fact, resignations and involuntary attrition can be opportunities to

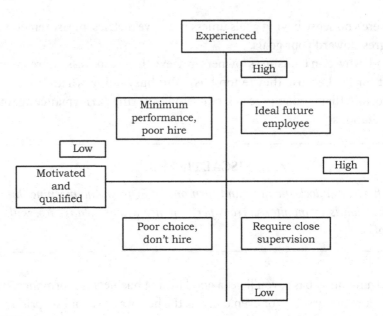

FIGURE 3.2
Hiring and motivation.

"cleanse" the organization and create brighter futures with better talent matches for growth needs.

Don't misunderstand: Employees are the most valuable asset of the business. Consequently, hiring the wrong people is one of the most serious of all errors. Your employees must be experienced, qualified, and motivated, as you can see in Figure 3.2.

1. If they're experienced and qualified but not motivated. You'll have *minimum performance*.
2. If they're qualified and motivated but not experienced, they'll require *close supervision and the tolerance for errors*.
3. If they're experienced and motivated but not qualified for future work, you'll have *a poor match of need and talent*.
4. This is your ideal future employee. How many of your current employees fit the criteria? (See the "SIR" method mentioned earlier—Sustain, Improve, Replace.)

The literature for two decades or more has been quite clear: Motivation is intrinsic—only self-generated—then it's maximized by employees being able to apply the widest range of their talents to a job *and being recognized for them.* That doesn't mean rewarding only victories, it means rewarding *positive behaviors.*

FISCAL FINESSE

Alan Weiss says: *If you give an unhappy employee more money, you'll then have a wealthier, unhappy employee.*

Provide your employees with the three outcomes you expect every month, obtain their commitment (or modifications), and then hold them to it. *Every month.* Be specific. "Take care of inventory" is meaningless, but "Keep inventory breakage to under 10 percent of total inventory" is very clear and measurable. In this way, you won't have to micro-manage anyone.

Help them to grow. When they ask, "Can you tell me what to do in this instance?" ask them, "First tell me what *you* think should be done." Don't do their jobs for them, help them to do their jobs.

EXCESSIVE OVERHEAD WILL DOOM YOU

Nothing is as deadly for business growth (or even survival) as excessive debt, and nothing creates excessive debt as fast as payroll.

This is a huge dilemma for growing businesses because of the build staff/grow or grow/build staff "chicken and egg" phenomenon.

For example, you say to yourself that you're going to increase your revenue by 10 percent by hiring three new salespeople. The three new salaries from hiring these salespeople now turn your business unprofitable. Generally speaking, *it takes at least three months for a new salesperson to get acclimated to a new job and start producing results.* Therefore, you face the reality of losing money for at least the next three months or perhaps longer. This is a prime example of too much payroll expense for your business.

Make an organization chart to give you a visual representation of your business. In addition to their names in the box, place the employee's total compensation alongside. This exercise helps you to understand if you're getting the return that you anticipated from that employee's efforts.

FISCAL FINESSE

ROI applies to your individual employees, not just your investment in the business as a whole.

Another area to be aware of as you grow your business is the cost of your office space. Opt for the less extravagant over the luxury office space. These resources can be better spent on your sales and marketing efforts. There will be plenty of time for more elegant office space (and maybe even a new company headquarters) after you've successfully grown your business.

Along with the expense of office space comes the additional investment in office furniture. Brand-new office furniture is a want, not a must. *It will not lead to increased sales for your business.* Use this capital instead for your sales and marketing efforts. There will come a time in the future for new office furniture.

As for free lunches, massages, snacks, and other perquisites, find the happy medium for your pocketbook.

Too much overhead when trying to grow your business is like having a 100-pound pack on your back. You can never get to full speed.

NOT ENOUGH WORKING CAPITAL (CASH AND/OR FINANCING) TO FUND YOUR GROWTH

Many small business owners ask the question, "How fast can I grow my business?" The simple answer to this question is, "It depends on how much capital you have." I will use the example of a boot strapped service company.

You start your business with $10,000. You buy a desk, a chair, and a computer. You land two new clients, which means that you're making enough money to pay your overhead, pay yourself, and still have a little left over. Congratulations, you're on your way! You land two more clients. Then, you find that you can't handle all of the work by yourself anymore, and you need to hire some help. You do that. You're still able to pay your overhead, pay yourself, pay your help, and still have money left over. Your small business is growing and you're managing your growth in the most desirable way possible!

As you probably may have learned, business is not perfect. Unexpected things happen along the way that throw the best-laid plans off track. For example, you have four clients and an employee, and you're doing just fine. But, in an instant, one of your clients goes away! Now, you're not making enough money to pay your overhead, yourself, and your employees. *It's the loss of that one client that caused your business to start losing money.* Instead of your business creating new money (profit) every month as it did in prior months, now your business needs new money (investment) in order to survive.

FISCAL FINESSE

To quote boxing champion Mike Tyson, "Everybody has plans until they get hit for the first time."

Now, the mad scramble begins to find a new client to replace the old one who just left. The pressure on you is great, because you have that overhead and payroll to meet each month. You figure that it will take at least a month to find a new client, so you use the cash that you have on hand for payroll and pay your overhead using your credit card. One month passes and you don't land that new client yet. So, you pay for your overhead by using your credit card again. You mumble to yourself, "This is no way to live."

Now your credit card is maxed out and you're feeling tremendous pressure to land that new client (this example is how most small businesses fail—because of lack of capital). So, how did you solve the problem? You did what every successful entrepreneur does. You went out and borrowed money from friends and family, or you obtained a new credit card, or you acquired that new client, finally. Countless entrepreneurs face this struggle time and time again. *The key to success is to keep your overhead as low as you possibly can, so you can live to fight another day.*

Well, you say, that's no fun! I need my $3,000 Mac computer, my $1,000 office chair, my $5,000 per month office space, my $1,000 per month Range Rover lease payment, my $3,000 per month home mortgage, my office snacks and sodas, and a healthy travel and entertainment budget. No, you really don't. By expanding your overhead at a faster rate than your sales are growing, you're putting yourself in a position of weakness. You're not leaving yourself any type of cushion in your growing business. As a matter of fact, you have now become the biggest threat facing your business. It's ok, you say, my pipeline looks good and I'll land more new clients next month.

You must avoid the natural tendency *to start spending money that you don't have.* One thing is certain: You know exactly how much your expenses are in any given month. *The thing that is uncertain is how much revenue you will generate in any given month.* By keeping your overhead as low as possible, you can reinvest your profits into growing your business.

Otherwise, you will be on the never-ending chase for finding more money.

Before we conclude, let me add some powerful social proof. When the pandemic hit in 2020 and the ensuing years, the individuals, small businesses, and large businesses which survived—and even thrived—had cash on hand. They were not in serious debt and didn't have to borrow. That's what low overhead and revenues exceeding expenses, and hard cash can do—guide you through volatility and disruption.

As it is, about 60 percent of all new businesses fail within five years, and another 60 percent of the survivors fail over the next five years. Keep your overhead as low as possible.

NOT TALKING TO YOUR CUSTOMERS ABOUT WHAT THEIR NEEDS ARE (TESTING THE MARKET)

While providing quality products and services is essential to having a successful business, ensuring that your business is aligned with your customers' needs is just as important for business growth. Your customers are the lifeblood of your business. Therefore, business owners must ensure that they know who their customers are, incorporate customer feedback, and train their team to effectively handle customer needs.

There's nothing worse than offering a product or service to customers who are uninterested. Knowing who your customers are—along with what they need—will help you put value in the product or service that

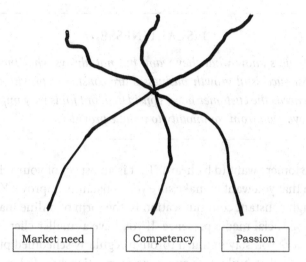

| Market need | Competency | Passion |

FIGURE 3.3
The essentials of an effective market presence.

you're offering. Understanding your customers will help to strengthen your brand and promote sales within your business.

In Figure 3.3, you can see the basic element.

- If you have competence running your business, and are passionate about it, but have no market need, you have a message that no one hears.
- If you have passion and market need, but no competence, the competition will be far ahead of you.
- If you have market need and competence, but no passion, you won't be resilient enough to overcome inevitable setbacks.

Where those three lines intersect represents powerful brand potential for your growth.

Incorporating customer feedback is one of the best things you can do for your business. This type of feedback is invaluable, as it allows you to see what's effective and what's not. Customer feedback will help guide your business to success, because this means that you can stay abreast of what your customers want, ultimately giving you a competitive edge.

FISCAL FINESSE

All customers know what they want, but not always what they need. The most successful growth businesses are constantly providing solutions to needs the customer never considered, but finds very important. That moves you from commodity to unique provider.

Your customers want to be heard. That is an aspect of your relationship with them that you want to make sure you constantly improve. You can do that through constant communication in the form of online mailing lists and a strong social media presence. If you have a smaller client base, you can make sure you stay in touch through regularly scheduled phone calls and meetings that build on your ongoing relationship. Following these practices will allow the customers to voice any concerns they may have, which could potentially allow you to improve the goods and services that you offer ahead of the competition.

UNDERPRICING YOUR PRODUCTS OR SERVICES

There is a time and a place for a low-priced product or service. But an underpriced product or service hurts your business for many reasons.

- Underpricing leads to lower margins for your business. We've already discussed the hazards of overhead, and low margins are equally dangerous. You can't make this up on volume!
- Underpricing leads to a perception of lesser value. People buy Brioni suits not because they are essential for attire, but because of the emotional appeal and status. Bentleys aren't necessary for transportation, and Bulgari watches are not essential to tell the time.[2]

FISCAL FINESSE

People believe, deep down, that they get what they pay for. Given three products with which the customer is not familiar when they want high quality, the tendency is to purchase the most expensive as an "assurance" of high quality.

- Underpricing leads to a perception of lower quality which may damage your brand. No one expects the people selling knock-off pocketbooks on street corners to have a product that's going to last a long time. But these people aren't reliant on repeat business and have no overhead!
- You will have to sell more units of a low-priced product if you're pursuing a high-growth strategy. Ten $10,000 dollar sales are not as lucrative as one $100,000 sale. That also applies to low-priced items. It's more expensive to sell more units.

Having covered the eight growth mistakes, let's turn to the more positive: the critical three aspects that accelerate growth safely.

NOTES

1 I learned this from Alan Weiss and his book, *Sentient Strategy: How to create market-dominating strategies in turbulent economies* (Routledge, 2023).
2 My nieces and nephews keep telling me I don't need a watch because I have the time on my phone. I keep telling them I don't wear a watch to tell the time.

4

The Three Aspects to Profitable Growth Sales

MORE "ACTIVE" CUSTOMERS (ACTUALLY BUYING YOUR GOODS AND SERVICES)

Your business currently has 50 active customers. In order to grow your sales, your goal is to add two more "active" customers. Not all prospects are alike, as we've shown in Figure 4.1.

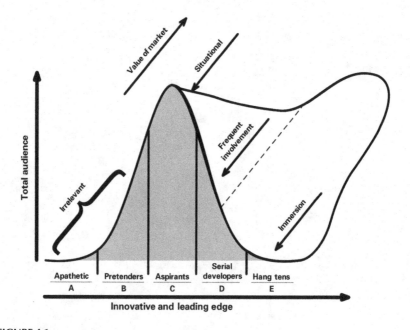

FIGURE 4.1

The range of quality customers. Blog Post by Alan Weiss, "Business of Consulting," November 18, 2011, alanweiss.com, reprinted with permission.

DOI: 10.4324/9781032710983-4

As you can see, your total audience might be large, but the qualitative buyers tend toward the left, so we've made this a three-dimensional figure. "Hang ten" is a surfing term, referring to the people who hang their toes over the front of the board to have a more thrilling ride. As you move from left to right, you find prospective customers who are very conservative, pay "lip service" to buying, watch what others do, and lead the way. The last two segments are the vital ones for "active" customers.

FISCAL FINESSE

You're better off with 500 high quality, targeted buyers than 5,000 indifferent prospects.

Your best prospects are those who believe in your "calling," have a clear need for your products and services, and have the means to purchase them. (As a side note, the people and organizations with money on hand were those who fared best during the pandemic.)

Why do we use "active"? Because these customers will:

- Make repeat purchases
- Not be price sensitive
- Refer others to you
- Virtually never complain
- Provide you with ideas for products and services.

Anyone who believes that "everyone is a prospect" doesn't understand the importance of focusing precious time and money on marketing to the very highest potential clients and customers.

So the first of the three aspects of growth sales is to identify and then create customers who are continually "active." In a store, you should see them often. Remotely, you should hear from them often. And they should readily respond when you seek them out.

This exercise may be considered the most challenging and expensive of the three methods, because it's tough to find new customers, as we established at the outset.

We also have to include "customer acquisition cost." How much does it cost you—we spoke of scarce time and money—to acquire a new customer? You have to be acutely aware of "closing time," which is the duration from the first contact with a prospect to the time that prospect spends money and becomes a customer.

This concept is known as "total days to cash" (TDTC). We show the phases in Figure 4.2. Let's say you're paid in advance, as some of us are for professional services. That is a negative TDTC: We are collecting money prior to incurring any expenses.

If "net 30" is your practice, but you provide the product or service immediately, then your TDTC is 30, which is in the red zone. If the customer has a policy of not paying for 30 days beyond that (or is inefficient), you're approaching the black zone. And if you're only paid when services are completed or the products have been used for 90 days, well, you may never be paid. You'll see that the longer you wait, the less leverage you have to speed up payments!

How much is the cost of your marketing, your lead generation, and your meeting expenses? How much is that cost relative to the profit that

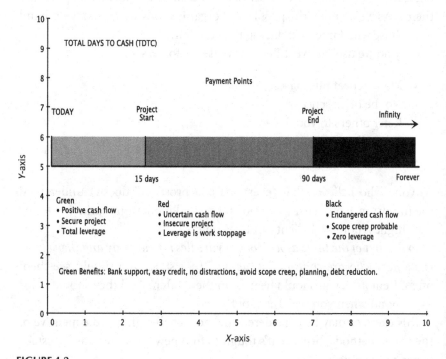

FIGURE 4.2
Total days to cash. From *The Business Wealth Builder*, Phil Symchych and Alan Weiss, Business Expert Press, 2016.

the new customer will provide to you in the first year? Does it make financial sense?

You have to perform a return-on-investment (ROI) analysis on your customers. We've described the types you should pursue in Figure 4.1. But what if you've made a mistake or you're setting your sights too low?

This is why you have to triage customers periodically to understand *how active they are*. We'll cover this in the ensuing segments in this chapter, but be sensitive to the fact that business increases in revenues when customers actively buy, when their frequency of purchase increases, and when the amount of the purchase increases. (We're not talking about other aspects such as referrals here, solely about a customer contributing to growth sales.)

What did it take to bring a new customer on board?

- Time required
- Number of interactions

What has the customer provided in terms of activity?

- Immediate new business
- Short-term repeat business

How does the customer compare to current, active customers?

- Equal at the same point in time, better, or worse
- Frequency and average spending increasing, stable, or decreasing

A great many businesses take pride in their customer or client list. But the question is whether those are active clients engaged in purchases, or "shadow" clients who emerge irregularly, or past clients with whom you haven't done business in months (or even years).

When you look at a firm's client list on the internet (or you consider the individuals on your own mailing list), ask how many would even talk readily with you today, much less place an order. "Quality" refers to *ongoing* interaction.

You can't pay the mortgage with money from non-active clients because they're no longer providing you with business!

ACTIVE CUSTOMERS BUYING MORE FREQUENTLY

Your business has 50 active customers. In total, these 50 active customers account for $5 million in sales. That's $100,000 per customer, which makes it easy.

Let's say that each customer makes one annual purchase.

The question about frequency is, what can we do to entice them to buy from us more than once a year. If you can make this happen, the growth in sales will fall largely to the bottom line, minus only your costs of product, delivery, commissions, and development.

By "development" we mean the time it takes to encourage a second and even a third purchase. Let's use an auto example.

Someone purchases a $100,000 car. (In 2018, there were 12 models that sold in the US for $100,000 or more. At this writing, five years later, there are 32.) Is there an opportunity to sell another vehicle for:

- Children going away to college
- The summer home, which is an airplane ride away
- A spouse or partner, so no more vehicle sharing is required
- A sports car for fun and as a hobby
- A pickup to haul the animals around or buy garden supplies
- A commuter so that it can be parked anywhere without worrying about damage.

You get the idea. The salesperson for that original purchase should be staying on top of family growth, new objectives, new needs, and new trends.

What if it isn't a product? After all, very big-ticket items such as medical imaging devices are not going to be sold more than once a year, if that, to the same customer. Now, let's look at a large insurance policy.

It could be that same year more insurance is needed because:

- There's been a dramatic increase in family income
- Age is bringing the possibility of increased, expensive illnesses
- Estate planning requires insurance to pay for estate taxes
- Disability is a more and more likely possibility
- The family has grown in size
- The business also requires insurance.

Other services would include legal, banking, design, accounting, home maintenance, lawn and tree care, and so forth. Our lawn care services include lawn mowing, shrub maintenance and fertilization, tree fertilizing and pruning, tick treatments, mulching, and so forth. In the winter, snow plowing, shoveling the walks and steps, and salting icy spots.

A grand example of this was the once-solely large accounting firms moving into consulting work. You can only prepare taxes once a year, but if you've established trust, why not provide additional services, such as consulting, coaching, and training? That's exactly what the huge accounting practices have done, such as McKinsey, Bain, Deloitte, and so forth.

Once clients trust you, they will be more likely to both buy the same value more than once *and also purchase additional offers of value.*

This requires innovation and constant contact with your clients.

FISCAL FINESSE

"Transporting trust" means to use a trusting relationship to provide more diverse products and services to the same client.

ACTIVE CUSTOMERS SPENDING MORE IN EACH TRANSACTION

We've identified that your 50 active customers spend $100,000 in each transaction. But what if you could get your active customers to spend $110,000 per transaction instead?

If you can do this, you just caused an increase in sales in your business.

Of course, you're wondering, "But how can I get them to do that? Easier said than done."

Here's how you *don't* do it: Don't tell them you're passing on your higher costs to them. They expect you to manage our business better than that. And don't tell them that it's been a long time since you raised prices, so it's the time to do so now. You're therefore punishing your longest-standing, most loyal customers.

FISCAL FINESSE

Existing customers shouldn't subsidize new customer acquisition. They should feel that they're getting the best "deal."

As we've noted, people don't like to pay more money, but they are even unhappier about passing up perceived higher value. So you must realize by now that *the key to this third aspect is to raise perceived value, not prices or fees.*

Some time ago, Poland Spring put handles on their cooler bottles so that they're easier to lift. However, I also noticed that the bottles were a gallon less than before. I challenged this. They told me the "convenience" was worth the extra money, but I told them not at the cost of 20 percent less product.

Poland Spring should have been more truthful, and not assumed its customers were idiots.

How we can raise perceived value:

- Provide longer support for the product;
- Provide examples of related usages;[1]
- Provide faster and more responsive help: have live "chats" on our website, not automated responses; return phone calls within a day or, better yet, have enough staff to have humans pick up the phone; reply to all email within a day with personalized responses, not boilerplate or ChatGPT;
- Provide a longer and better return policy;
- Provide discounts for frequent buyers who spend a certain minimum;
- Share surveys showing you're at or near the top of the industry;
- Assign a personal representative or phone contact if possible.

You don't need a huge increase in the average transaction, especially if you have a healthy volume of customers.

KEY TAKEAWAYS

These are the three ways to grow sales. Everything else is a sub-strategy of one of these three primary strategies. The common denominator of these three aspects is that you must learn how to sell. The art of selling is certainly one of the things that you will want to study and master.

Marketing is the creation of need and selling is the provision of goods and services which meet that need. You can be commodity-based, selling on volume and low prices, or quality based, selling on brand, uniqueness, and emotional appeal.

In general, people expect to get what they pay for. That means that the ego-building and pride of wearing a Brioni or driving a Bentley easily justify the prices that are not really necessary for comfortable attire or safe transportation.

FISCAL FINESSE

Alan Weiss says: Logic makes people think, but emotion makes them act.

All three aspects can be applied at once, since they all have specific benefits: keeping customers actively engaged, increasing purchase frequency, and increasing investment in each transaction. These are not difficult concepts. Clothiers do it readily by offering different attire based on the season, latest fashions, and new materials.

The greatest tool of all, in my experience, is called customer relationship management. This is often referred to as "CRM" and connected to specific technologies, *but the concept is important and can be conducted without using any particular methodology.*

In terms of overview, one can gain insights about existing customers utilizing telephone conversations, email, Zoom, meetings, sales histories, referrals provided, and so forth. Depending on the type of business, social media may or may not be useful, and only then in limited degrees in conjunction with other types of information gathering and analysis.

(As an aside, this process is also useful for former customers as well as potential customers, but here we're discussing only current customers.)

The concept originated about a half-century ago (surprising, right?) when "customer focused" was popular and customer satisfaction a key performance area. (Since then, we've come to realize some of the weaknesses of those beliefs because the customer *is not* always right!)

The advent of modern computing and the "cloud" has made this much easier and more effective. But our suggestion is to be as industry-specific as possible and oriented toward your ideal buyer as much as possible (see Figure 4.1).

Further, customer relationship management changes as your customers mature, change, and evolve. So whether you utilize some form of technology or not, your personal understanding of your best customers and your strategy for the future are the most important elements in effective CRM.

Here are some varied components of CRM as shown in Figure 4.3.

Especially as a startup, choose elements which are simple and frequent, such as verbal communication, the internet, classifying your customers, and the direct feedback of your marketing and sales efforts. Since you're wearing those varied "hats" we discussed earlier, you don't have to wait for reports from people who are too busy to provide them!

Make no mistake, you're not wasting time focusing on the status and responsiveness of your customer base no matter what stage of development your business is transiting.

A client or customer's value can be calculated through an analysis of these data points. We discussed above that a great deal of this is observational and anecdotal, not dependent on "Big Data" or sophisticated computing. A simple spreadsheet can tell you about a customer's value.

FIGURE 4.3

Varied aspects of CRM. Ali Feizbakhsh Tavana, Saeed Fili, Alireza Tohidy, Reza Vaghari, Saed Kakouie "Theoretical Models of Customer Relationship Management in Organizations." *International Journal of Business and Behavioral Sciences.* Vol. 3, No. 11, November 2013.

Here are some ideas for your evaluation, although you may have far better ones depending on the nature of your business.

- What did it cost to bring them aboard (onboarding)?[2]
- What does it cost to sustain them (deals, discounts, and responsiveness)?
- How many referrals do they provide when asked?
- How many referrals do they provide unasked?
- What is their frequency of purchase?
- What is the amount of their average purchase?
- What is the duration of their purchasing?

We call the combination of these traits and practices "evergreen clients," and they can provide you with business no matter what the "seasonal or climatic conditions" may be.

They don't drop their leaves and they don't drop you!

How do you look at a client? By the value of today's sale? If so, perhaps you're selling yourself short. Always take into consideration what the life-time value of a client is to your business.

We have had the following relationships:

- Lawn care: 12 years
- Personal physician: 17 years
- Favorite restaurant and weekly dinner: 20 years
- Auto brand: 18 years
- Dentist: 20 years
- Accountant: 20 years
- Attorney, litigator: 20 years
- Attorney, estate planning: 10 years
- Investment firm: 41 years.

I've had several clients of 15-year, 12-year, and 8-year durations.

Now think about this yourself: What products and services have you utilized for extended periods? What people have utilized your products and services for extended periods? Understand that you *have* engaged in this dynamic from both sides.

Why?

How can you make that client feel special, so that they remain loyal to your products and services? That's the magic of CRM. That's what's been done for you in many cases.

SOCIAL PROOF

This is the provision of examples that others can relate to in order to prove your point. We've tried to provide that in the bullet point examples above. We often ask people, "When was the last time you ordered something from a 'cold call' by telephone, or from a spammer?" (Mine was 1993, one of the first long-distance telephone services known as MCI.) If that's the case—it's rare or never happened—then why expect people will buy from you with those techniques?

You don't want to simply "sell business," nor "bring on board a client." You want to create a long-term *relationship* with that "evergreen client" who will support you through many years of mutually beneficial relationships.

Consequently, CRM is a factor of identifying, sustaining, nurturing, and capitalizing on these solid relationships by providing anticipated *and* unanticipated value. That's why those people above have been with us for so long. They don't just provide accounting help—they suggest new techniques to lower taxes, keep track of changing laws, and are sensitive to our changing family and personal situations. The doctor recommends new vaccines or discourages invalid treatments.

But growth and great clients don't occur without risk. Let's turn now to risk management.

NOTES

1 The company which sold and installed a client's emergency generators sends a newsletter monthly on energy-saving tips.
2 See *Onboarding Matters*, Donna Weber, Springboard Publishing, 2021.

5

Managing Risk

WHAT IS AN APPROPRIATE RATE OF GROWTH FOR MY BUSINESS?

Managing risk is an important part of being successful in your growth strategy. Sometimes, things happen that are completely unexpected and could not have been reasonably forecasted (like a natural disaster or a new government regulatory demand).

Let's first understand the two elements of risk:

- *Seriousness:* This is the gravity of the impact of the event occurring. A minor degree of seriousness might be a wasted day or a lost customer. A major degree might be a plant shutdown or a horrible review in the media.
- *Probability:* This is the likelihood of a given risk occurring. Low probability means that it would be unusual or rare, such as twice a year. We've all heard of "hundred-year storms" for example. High probability means the event is almost guaranteed to occur, such as a new employee making a mistake or a chronically unhappy customer making a complaint.

That leaves us with four possibilities:

1. **Low seriousness and low probability**: You can probably ignore these risks, such as a major earthquake in New York or snow in June.
2. **Low seriousness but high probability**: You need to have some actions prepared to deal with this. Slipping on ice in the winter isn't at all unusual. We should take steps to eliminate ice buildup on our driveways and sidewalks, and also have a first aid kit handy.

DOI: 10.4324/9781032710983-5

3. **High seriousness and low probability**: In the United States, the rate of 0.18 fatal accidents per one million flights since 2017 is impressive. You still hear the safety announcements on every flight, and overwater aircraft have life jackets and rafts. A large meteor hitting the Earth is an example. One such encounter wiped out the dinosaurs, but it hasn't happened again in 66 million years.

4. **High seriousness and high probability**: This requires that we not only try to prevent the occurrence but are also prepared to deal with it when it almost inevitably occurs anyway. Bad winter weather will delay or cancel flights. Contagious diseases will inhibit work and family life. Deaths occur in all families and all businesses.

FISCAL FINESSE

People love to take action. But unless we take risk management into account, we're jumping on a wagon racing downhill that doesn't have any brakes.

We've been talking about two kinds of actions to take regarding the seriousness and probability elements of risk: preventive and contingent.

Preventive actions are intended to reduce the probability of an adverse event occurring: putting up "no smoking" signs, isolating combustible materials, having a fire marshal inspection, and so forth. **Contingent** actions are intended to mitigate the effects of an adverse event: sprinklers, fire extinguishers, insurance, escape routes, and so forth.

Note that effective preventive action prevents injury, loss of life, financial loss, and embarrassment. Contingent action is only effective after the problem has already arisen.

Now that we've specified the elements of risk and its prevention and mitigation, let's look at some specifics related to your business.

One of the main ways to de-risk your growth strategy is to maintain a rate of growth that works for you. You don't have to try to grow your company by 100 percent every year. Keep in mind that if you could grow your business profitably 5 percent a year forever, your company would be a Wall Street superstar!

Remember the Alan Weiss example: If you improve your business by just 1 percent a day (or improve yourself or your employees), in 70 days you'd be twice as good as you are now!

Thus, gradual and incremental growth can be quite dramatic.

We've mentioned earlier not to use other people's metrics. Look at your financing, your market, your talents, and your resources, then decide what constitutes positive, lower risk, yet acceptable growth. If you exceed that, fine. But this is one of the reasons we highlighted "bootstrapping" earlier and advised not taking on outside investors who will want very high and very rapid growth and profits.

If you're doing very well, you can always adjust your growth projections upwards. Remember about "playing with house money." But if you're too ambitious, you can't easily reduce your goals once you've already expended the money and resources.

How do you calculate the appropriate rate of growth for your business? There are two ways to make this calculation. One is a simple approach and the other is a little more complicated.

Here's the simple approach: Based on your existing profitability, calculate how much of these profits you would be able to apply toward your growth strategy. What percentage of these profits do you think you can use? You need to look at your financial situation and make the decision.

You don't want to use all of your profits, just a portion of them. *You don't want to use so much of your profits for your growth strategy that you make your business unprofitable.* This is where many business owners get hung up. You must be able to maintain profitability, while you grow your business at a measured rate.

You'll need profits to deal with (beyond growth):

- Unexpected events (repairs, legal issues, taxes, and so on)
- Salary, bonuses, expense reimbursement, and hiring
- Technology improvements and repairs
- Advertising, media, and public relations (PR).

Thus, you can't just plow profits back into growth, because the upper stories will collapse if the foundation weakens.

The other approach is a little more complicated: Use a financial projection model. Load up your growth assumptions, and then your financial model will calculate for you what percentage rate of growth would trigger a borrowing need. That percentage would be the highest percentage that your business could grow without having to borrow money. You might need a financial person to help you with this one, and it will have much higher accuracy for your detail-oriented types.

Most growing firms, when successful, aren't prepared for success and simply keep trying to grow. If you're familiar with the board game *Monopoly*, you know that you can't simply buy every property on which you land because you'll quickly run out of the money you need to pay rent to others when you land on their properties, to buy houses, to pay taxes, and even to get out of jail!

So, blindly and constantly investing in more hires, more products, more services, more advertising, and so forth doesn't necessarily get you growth, but can get you mired in debt.

And debt, here, is a fork in the road.

GROW WITH LESS DEBT; NOT MORE DEBT

If managed carefully, debt can be your friend. If not, debt will become the enemy of your business. Do your best to use debt sparingly as you grow your business.

Using debt is not immoral or illegal. We use it for mortgages, major purchases, tuition, and even incidental shopping. *But the key is to undertake debt that you're certain you can repay.* Your monthly mortgage payments are accommodated in your cash flow (they had better be!). The same for car payments or even restaurant meals. One of the great problems in these times is that using debt for college tuition was done *without* a reasonable certainty of paying it back. If you are a philosophy or European literature major, you're probably not going to get a job after graduation that can easily pay back $300,000 of debt. You can go to a less expensive school, or change your major and focus on a different career. *But you can't incur $300,000 of debt if you know you're going to be earning only $50,000 annually, unless you intend to live in your parents' basement or rob a bank.*

What is the biggest problem with borrowing money? You have to pay it back! That's an old joke I was taught when I worked as a corporate banker. There's truth to it!

We've all heard about people maxing out their credit cards to pay other credit cards each month. But debt entails *interest* ("vigorish" in the vernacular) and that keeps growing. Look at the required legal disclaimer on your credit card bills: If you make only the minimum payment per month of, say, $18,000, you'll be paying it for 20 years and wind up paying $54,000 over that time period.

That's no way to stay fiscally prudent.

FISCAL FINESSE

The idea is not to avoid debt, but to use it wisely and prudently with the intent of paying it off with a clear and short-term plan.

People generally don't pay off mortgages quickly, but they do accommodate the payments in their cash flow, can generally deduct the interest from their taxes, and own an appreciating asset through that investment.

Your business is no different. Use debt wisely and judiciously in order to grow, but don't allow it to use you.

Another joke I was taught in banking: No one ever went out of business from having too much debt. It was the inability to service that debt that caused their demise. That's like saying that it's not the fall from a tall building that kills you, it's the sudden stop!

The key consideration about debt is that it has to be paid off, usually with interest and even penalties. A great many students thought the government was going to erase their student debt, but they were wrong. Even debt in a family that's "forgiven" can create ill will and resentment. And that debt didn't disappear; someone else paid it off.

Borrow for the short term, for example, to hire a new salesperson who will be productive short term and enable you to quickly pay back the loan, or to improve your technology so that customers can order online faster and in greater quantities.

Don't borrow for ego or "show." If customers don't come to you, then you don't need fancy offices, furniture, or artwork. (If you can afford these in the normal cash flow of a successful enterprise, fine.) Don't borrow for "safety." Even if you put the money in the bank "in case you need it," you're still paying interest on it and your credit score will reflect the outstanding debt, which could hurt your future borrowing and interest rates.

Debt is often alluringly simple. Credit cards inform you of your cash available to borrow. Shady operations offer "instant credit" (often at confiscatory rates). *Use debt proactively, not out of desperation.*

Finally, a banker will always lend you his umbrella when it is sunny outside. When you need a loan, they're very hard to get. When you don't need a loan, banks (and other financial institutions) line up with tantalizing offers.

These jokes are actually lessons in disguise. You spend all of this time and endure all of this stress to build your business. Imagine that you end up losing your business because you made a mistake somewhere or something unexpected happened (see COVID-19) that caused you to default on your bank debt.

The people and organizations which made it best through COVID-19 were those which had cash. Assets didn't have to be sold and loans didn't have to be sought. There was hard cash, which went a long way.

My father used to say, "Them that has, gets." He meant that the more assets you have and the more wealth you accrue, the more assets you'll acquire and the more your wealth will build. Risk management involves the careful parsing out of what you need for safety and what you need for growth. These are not antithetical, but rather synergistic. You grow best when you're in a strong position, not when you have your hat in your hand in line at the bank.

Use a portion of the profits that you earn to reinvest in your business for growth. Use a bank line of credit to finance the carry of your accounts receivable. That's because, assuming you have good, solid clients who run their businesses as we recommend here that you run your business, they're "good for the money." You may find a family illness or natural disaster may delay the payments of an otherwise fine client. So, debt can be used to "finance" or carry income which isn't available as expected, *but is going to arrive somewhat late*.

And remember our earlier discussion and illustration about total days to cash (TDTC). You want to minimize this as much as possible, but you still may find some customers delinquent.

The takeaway here is to use borrowed funds judiciously!

SOMETIMES BUILDING A BETTER MOUSETRAP CAN BE MORE SUCCESSFUL WITH LESS RISK

Remember, history has shown that building a better mousetrap can be wildly successful. Uber debuted as merely a better taxi service—scheduled rides, billed to a personal account, rating drivers, clean cars, drivers who knew where they were going, and constant status on a smartphone.

Dyson didn't invent vacuum cleaners, but rather improved the airflow for more effective cleaning (and hair drying, and hand sanitizing).

FedEx didn't invent package delivery, but did create a hub-and-spoke method to enable next-day service.

Apple didn't invent computers, but rather made them both easy to use and cosmetically attractive.

These are all manifestations of *conformist innovation*, meaning they improved what already existed. The first person who decided to eat an oyster is to be commended for originality and daring. The person eating the "oyster tower" in a high-end restaurant is not.

Creating original and brand-new products and services is not only laudable but also expensive, time consuming, and risky. The probability of going into debt is, consequently, very high.

A product or service that simply improves on what already is accepted and exists may not be so thrilling or exotic, but it is a far more prudent risk and provides the opportunity to manage growth and risk with far less need to incur debt.

FISCAL FINESSE

It was much safer to develop apps for smartphones after the first ones proved reliable and attractive to buyers. Amazon's amazing distribution system was validated when the company was "merely" selling books through it.

You don't necessarily have to try to create something new in the world to have a successful business. The Wright Brothers weren't the first people in flight. But they were the first people in *powered* flight.

There are dreamers, of course—a few of whom have been successful— who created something totally new which took the world (or at least the market) by storm. But for every such success, there have been 100,000 failures. Electric, rented scooters have been all the rage in many cities, but we're seeing their demise because of safety issues, damaged and lost (and stolen) scooters, and complaints of their aesthetic repugnance lying on street corners.

Plus, creating something new in the world usually takes a significant amount of time, effort, and capital with no guarantee of success. You're a business person, not a gambler.

The question is this: What is your passion, your "calling"? What enables you to quickly be consumed by value you're offering, so that your work is

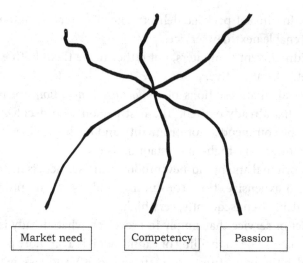

| Market need | Competency | Passion |

FIGURE 5.1
Three dynamics for new product/service success.

not onerous but rather an ongoing challenge? *Is this something that you can convert into a business?*

Let's be clear: You can't simply turn a hobby into a career. Stamp collecting or hiking or bird-watching or model-building may be intensely rewarding personally, but that does not a career make.

But if you've successfully coached people (to be better athletes, or speakers, or caregivers), that can become a full-time business. If you've repaired watches or model trains or fireplaces, those also can become businesses.

As noted in Chapter 3, we need three major components to create viable products and services to market (Figure 5.1).

What are you passionate about? Is there something that you enjoy doing that you can improve upon? In Figure 5.1, you can see the three complementary traits of a successful market presence.

> **Market need**: That is the need you can identify (faster service), anticipate (incorporating new technology), or create (remote team meetings).
> **Competency**: The skills, traits, and behaviors required to do the job better than anyone else.
> **Passion**: Your "calling" which is responsible for your motivation and commitment (and hard work).

If you have market need and competency, but no passion, you simply have a nine-to-five job, even if you own the place.

If you have market need and passion but no competency, you'll lose out to more competent competitors.

If you have competency and passion but no market need, you have a story no one wants to hear.

Where these three routes intersect should be your brand.

Most customers and clients know what they *want* but not what they *need*. I never knew I needed a car phone (pre-smartphones) until a salesperson demonstrated the advantages. I never knew I needed a TV remote or automatic garage door opener until I tried them. *A need is special, a luxury fulfilled, until used once. After that, it becomes a necessity.*

Your passion enables you to take on otherwise onerous responsibilities and do them well, without complaint and with careful attention. That's why you'd prefer employees who are passionate about the kind of work you do, because they'll act in the same manner.

Perhaps, there's something that you can make more efficient. You don't need to be a creative genius. Pick something that you are familiar with and that you have an interest in. As a result of the pandemic, even high-end restaurants realized that take-out orders and home delivery would remain popular. That has greatly increased profitability because there are no expenses involved with tableware, linens, servers, and so forth.

We all want to be effective, but efficiency is about being effective with a minimum of waste, unneeded actions, and errors. Having roadside assistance if you have car trouble is very effective, but if it requires a three-hour wait, it's not very efficient.

If you feel that you must create a new product or service, then by all means, create! Keep in mind that your risks will be much larger, as will your capital requirements. Consider that most successful products and services are incremental. That is, they are improvements over the past, but not radically new ideas.

Even on a large scale, Uber is simply a better taxi service. FedEx is a better delivery service. Dyson is a better air movement business.

Thus, improving your technology to allow customers to buy more, or order faster, or make suggestions is of high value. Providing next-day delivery opportunities can be a "breakthrough" for people.

Starbucks initiated both ordering ahead and immediate pickup with no lines needed at the stores, *and a "walk-thru" akin to a drive-thru for people to walk up and make a purchase.* How much are you focusing on making it easier for your customers to browse, order, receive deliveries, return products, ask questions, make recommendations, give you positive reviews, and so forth?

The point here is to choose what works for you. It's not always necessary to create something "new" in order to be successful in business. You can still be successful in business by expanding on an existing idea and simply building a better mousetrap.

Or a better buying experience.
Or an easier payment system.
You get the idea?

THE INSURANCE YOU NEED AND DON'T NEED

Find a quality insurance broker and get only the insurance you need and enough of it. Don't try to find insurance yourself. A good broker, who represents many firms and not just one (as most agents represent just one company), is the best bet. And the best way to find a good broker is to ask people who have one. Talk to other small business owners, members of the chamber of commerce, and so forth. Ask for a broker who represents many different companies.

You don't necessarily want the cheapest insurance any more than you'd want the cheapest heart surgeon. You want *appropriate and effective* insurance, which we'll discuss shortly. Some insurance plans will require that all employees also be covered, and insurance benefits are an excellent tool to attract and retain top talent.

Some policies and coverage will be mandatory; some will be up to you. *The maximum amount of insurance isn't necessarily the best for you.* That's why you need a broker who can consider your company and its situation. Most insurance can be adjusted as needed, so long as a certain minimum is maintained.

There are also some differences in coverage for purely product versus purely service firms. State requirements in the United States can also differ, and the volume of your business may affect premiums. Your broker can assist you in looking into claims experiences from various companies, including deductibles and riders.

As a business owner, some of the insurance you need is going to be mandatory, for example, worker's compensation insurance and commercial liability insurance. Some insurance depends on your time of business and willingness to accept risk. And some of it is dependent on your customers.

An example of this last point is that many major companies will not accept a contract from a consultant, coach, financial expert, or other source without a copy of the cover page of an in-force E&O policy ("errors and omissions," colloquially known as "malpractice"). Thus, you couldn't even be considered by those firms without evidence of such insurance. We live in a highly litigious society.

There are other types of insurance for you to consider personally, as well as for business, such as health insurance. You could take the risk and not carry health insurance on yourself. However, if you experience a medical problem, the financial impact could bankrupt you. Therefore, it's crazy not to have health insurance, especially since it can be paid for by your firm as a benefit for employees. (Remember that we specified earlier that some benefits must be available for *all* employees and could be construed as hiring incentives.) As your business grows and you add employees, you're definitely going to need health insurance as a basic recruiting tool to help you attract talent and be competitive in the marketplace.

Speaking of attracting talent, you may want to take a look at also adding group benefits insurance, which would include life insurance, long-term disability, and short-term disability. These plans provide valuable benefits, are cost-effective for your business, and help your recruiting efforts.

You're actually more likely to become disabled than to die. Those of you who are refugees from larger companies will realize that disability insurance was previously provided for you in a group policy, but now you must acquire one for yourself (or offer another group policy for your employees).

FISCAL FINESSE

Failing to obtain disability insurance is one of the most common errors of new businesses. And it can cost you a fortune if you don't.

Disability insurance can be quite expensive, *but the younger you are when you obtain it, the cheaper it is.* You want to be sure there is a 90-day waiting period (before benefits begin) which makes it even less expensive, *and that payments are not just made until you're able to work again, but rather until you're able to work in the exact same job again.* These policies usually pay about 80 percent of the salary being missed. That's why you should make sure you take a regular salary.

Depending on the nature of your business, you may be required to carry commercial liability insurance. This is different from E&O, in that it means if someone falls in your place of business, or cuts themselves on some product you provided, your commercial liability insurance will kick-in. Even if you're not directly involved (the problem was the landlord didn't clear the ice in front of the building where you're located) everyone in sight is usually sued.

You will also want to consider business interruption insurance. This can apply to natural disasters where the disaster itself, or the government's response to it, prevented you from reopening your business.

What you don't need as you're trying to grow your business and manage risk are the expensive premiums associated with whole life insurance policies. Your quality insurance broker will tell you that you can get term insurance instead and it is much more cost-effective. After you hit it big in your business, there will be plenty of money for you to buy whole life insurance policies if you desire. But they are neither good investments nor the best insurance policies.

Finally, a strong "risk umbrella policy" is highly important. This policy takes effect when you reach a limit of coverage with your other policies. If you're sued for a defective product causing damage in the amount of $3 million, and your liability coverage is only $2 million, the "umbrella" will pay the final million. Your insurance broker will recommend the dollar amount of umbrella insurance coverage based on your business's needs, and these premiums tend to be inexpensive.

You have choices about dental insurance, eye insurance, and even pet insurance, but you can see why a good broker is an important asset to set this all up.

Now let's talk more about how you pay for all of this.

6

Managing Your Business's Cash Cycle

CALCULATING YOUR CASH CYCLE

If your customers usually pay you in 45 days and your bills are due in 30 days, then you have a 15-day cash gap. How will you finance this gap? There are several ways to manage this challenge.

But first, think always about *terms*. If you decide your terms are, for example, "30 days, net," that bill isn't going to be paid in 30 days, but more probably in 60. Procurement and accounts payable on the business-to-business side, and consumers on the business-to-customer side, don't feel that an additional 30 days of delay will "hurt" anyone. Even property taxes and mortgage payments aren't considered delinquent (or reported to credit bureaus) unless they are 60–90 days overdue.

And probably no one is worried about you reporting them to a credit bureau. Be honest, would you even know how?!

What happens when you buy a dinner at a restaurant? You pay at the time (even if you use a credit card, the restaurant can collect immediately). The same for an auto loan. The auto dealer is paid in full by the bank financing your car. Major and minor purchases are paid at the time of the transaction in one way or another every day.

Consequently, we're recommending you at least consider "payment due on receipt of our invoice." That may mean a 30-day delay or it may create immediate payment, but it does mean you can begin to follow up on delayed payments far more quickly.

DOI: 10.4324/9781032710983-6

FISCAL FINESSE

*Some organizations have a rule (as do some nonprofits and govern-ment agencies) that any offered discount **must** be accepted. Hence, if you offer 5 percent off for payment within ten days, you have a very good chance of receiving it.*

Now let's consider methods other than billing practices to finance cash gaps.

If you qualify, a business line of credit is one way. You'll need to have excellent personal credit. In addition to a lien on some of your business assets, you will need to give your personal guarantee. You will almost always have something called a borrowing base, which limits the amount you can borrow to a percentage of your accounts receivable and finished goods inventory. A business line of credit is the cheapest form of financing because you don't need to give up ownership of any of your business. Find a good banker to help you, or an expert personal accountant or accounting firm.

It's always best to show the gap, demonstrate when excess cash is due to pay off the loan, and create excellent credit by so doing. Ironically, per-haps, the more you borrow and promptly repay, the better your credit score, enabling better borrowing in the future.

Another way to finance the cash gap is to require a larger up-front pay-ment at the time you invoice your customer. For example, if you're a ser-vice provider, you can ask for 50 percent, 30 percent, and 20 percent payment terms which are based on completion milestones.

But try this (take a deep breath): Why not make your standard profes-sional services contract a minimum of 50 percent as a deposit? (And a discount, as we've discussed, for full payment on acceptance.) Then create payment terms maximally beneficial to you. If you have to negotiate, you're negotiating from a very favorable position to begin with.

It's okay to negotiate terms, but never negotiate fees or prices. If you do that, the question quickly becomes, "How low will you go?"

Try to be paid in two or at most three installments. Monthly is never good, because it's far too simple for a customer to cease payment. The more money you've collected, the more leverage you have against future delayed payments, *by refusing to continue working or providing products and services*. And never accept a payment at "completion" because, for a great many customers, there will never be "completion!"

So try to be paid as much and as rapidly as possible. Remember our discussion of total days to cash. If that becomes too great, there will be fewer days to bankruptcy.

Be careful not to give off "deal vibes." Alan Weiss notes that he coaches a great many people who complain that disparate prospects all request a "deal" of some kind, such as an arbitrary price reduction, or highly extended terms, or even a delay of several months before any billing.

First, ask these deal-hungry prospects if they would agree to that with their own customers. If not, why would they expect you to provide it? If yes, then you're certainly not obligated to follow their poor business model.

Second, when this happens, the common factor is *you*. "Deal vibes" occur when you make concessions:

- Abrupt cancellation of a meeting
- Shortened time span at the last minute
- Granting a concession on request
- Extending return periods.

When you do these things, even unconsciously, you're manifesting a willingness to make nearly any concession to get the business. That's a "deal vibe" and it will readily expand to pricing and fees.

Alan Weiss talks about how he once talked to a prospect who would clearly become a client.

At the last minute, the prospect said, "Would you include another one of my employees in the deal?"

I asked why I should do that. "Because I have a streak of six years when everything I purchased included a price reduction or free products and services."

"Well, your streak is now over," I said. He signed.

Remember that once is an accident, twice is a coincidence, and three times is a pattern. That pattern is your creation if you give off "deal vibes." Don't easily make concessions. If the customer says, "I'm going to be two hours late for the appointment," don't allow it, reschedule.

All of this advice enables you to calculate your cash cycle with a high degree of accuracy, *unless you waver and don't hold your customers and clients to agreements, and unless you don't take a realistic view.* It's important to project cash cycles so that you can use debt intelligently, repay rapidly, and maintain a high credit score and reputation with your creditors.

PAYROLL AND OVERHEAD MUST BE PAID IN CASH

Cash is king and queen in business. In fact, it's the entire deck of cards. Financial success in business is based on timing, which means always having cash on hand when you need it.

When it became clear that the pandemic was going to be long and uncertain—along with its restrictions—many businesses called their bankers to ask for additional financing. Due to the high risks associated with lending money into an uncertain repayment scenario, many bankers refused to provide additional financing above and beyond what they were already legally committed to provide. That left many businesses in dire straits.

Think a bit to the major organizations, the small businesses, *and the individuals/entrepreneurs* you observed who made it best through the pandemic, not just surviving but actually thriving. Did they do it by going into debt? Did they close up and re-emerge? No. Almost all of them were able to do well because they had cash to pay off short-term debt, to invest in the business, to retain employees, *and to continue marketing.*

By "cash," we're talking about money in bank accounts,[1] readily converted stocks and bonds, and credit lines. We're not talking about hard-to-sell stocks, property, jewelry, collectibles, and the like. For those of you involved with nonprofits, this is especially true. Donors do not like to contribute to pay off debt, but rather toward growth.

It is important to note that cash is the lifeblood of every business. Even when interest rates are negligible (in Germany they charge you to keep your money in their banks!), you need to have cash on hand. When you have ready cash, you can pay your own vendors promptly, ensuring that you'll earn their loyalty and their priority time.

You'll be able to invest in incremental improvements in your business. That may not mean refurbishing the building or office, but it can mean local advertising or an expanded web initiative.

FISCAL FINESSE

It makes a difference when you pick up a check, far beyond that immediate meal.

Alan Weiss shared a story about why not to be penny wise and pound foolish.

"My wife and I were looking for our first house. A very nice, veteran realtor took us to lunch during our search one day. She saw a birthday cake served at a nearby table, and she asked the waiter to put the woman's drink on her bill. I immediately felt she was not only polite, but extremely successful. That lunch and drink probably cost about $20 back then, but I sent business her way whenever I could."

Alan's point: This realtor wasn't trying to save every penny, but rather to invest in her business. You can't invest without money in your pocket that you're not worried about spending. Play the long game.

You can't use your business's accounts receivable, inventory, and fixed assets to pay your employees and your landlord.

During hard times, assertive businesspeople invest to take advantage of their competition withdrawing and "belt-tightening." Your non-liquid assets can't assist you there. We're not talking about the proverbial "throwing good money after bad," but rather about the need to be strong enough to take advantage of volatile times when your competition becomes scared (or unable) to invest in their businesses.

As a rule of thumb, try to have six months of projected operating expenses in the bank in cash. By "projected," we're urging you not to simply consider your current expenditures extended out, but also likely new costs, such as planned hires, increased advertising, compensating for late payments by customers in hard times, and rising costs due to the economy. The peace of mind and resilience this fund provides more than offsets any additional return on the savings you could have achieved in the market.

A word here on alternative investments before we go on. If you're going to buy crypto (which seems at this point more of an investment than an alternative monetary source), or invest in a friend's startup, don't count that in your overall planning and saving. That's more like going to the casinos with a limit: If you win, great; but if you lose, chalk up the loss to entertainment and don't invest more trying to grab it back.

You're at your dinner table, not the Vegas tables.

Therefore, you need to pay close attention to the cash levels in your business.

If you have a CFO or an accountant who works closely with you on the outside, assign this as a priority task. You should know *daily* what your cash levels are. Just as most people check their stocks daily to understand their performance (and their real net worth), you need to have the discipline (or someone else's discipline) to know exact cash amounts, which can abruptly change.

Why "abruptly"? Because sometimes customers and clients are late paying—very late. Unexpected repairs are required. Insurance rates increase. Insurance installments you don't normally think about are due. You have to pay an unexpectedly high commission or bonus or give someone a raise to keep them from leaving. A customer puts a purchase sequence on "hold" or suddenly reduces the overall expenditure. Interest rates on savings fall or interest rates on mortgages increase. (The dangers of ARMs—adjustable rate mortgages.)

By knowing your cash levels on a constantly contemporary basis, you can better plan to delay or accelerate non-mandatory purchases and improvements. You know whether you can extend special terms or insist on your normal ones. You can delay or accelerate hires, and even accelerate debt repayment.

Since we all can become too embroiled in the details of our businesses, find an independent, outside professional to oversee cash flow analysis and reporting.

To return to our theme here, all salaries and cash benefits must be paid in cash. Once you skip a payroll, you're tumbling down a slippery slope. (Once again, this is even more critical for nonprofits.) This is why an incentive is quite appropriate to reduce total days to cash to zero (or even to a negative number—being paid prior to delivery of products and services). Providing a 5 percent discount today to have cash in your hands tomorrow is usually far superior to insisting on 100 percent, which may take many months to collect.

These same principles, of course, apply to our private lives. The discipline of intently tracking cash flow is universally useful. You can go into debt for that great vacation or a new car, but you'd better be able to forecast exactly when and how you'll pay it back.

If you don't think this is serious, consider the fiasco of college tuition debt. A presumptive history major who decides to attend an Ivy League school which will result in $300,000 of loans even after scholarships (if available) may wind up with a $45,000 starting teacher's salary. That will allow almost nothing after modest living expenses to pay down the debt.

A similar result occurs when you take out a 30-year home mortgage and end up repaying three times what you borrowed.

We need to be smarter than that.

A COMBINED 12-MONTH BUDGET AND CASH FLOW FORECAST GIVES YOU PLENTY OF FUTURE VISIBILITY

That way, you have plenty of time to act before an emergency cash situation presents itself.

Budgets are projections, and cash flow is a daily reality. Those should mesh, or cash flow should exceed budget, but you're in trouble *when cash flow is below budget*. The time to realize that is instantly, not a month later and not when you suddenly have to use your credit lines or delay payments.

Find an easy template online that you like to use. There are hundreds of examples available online because everyone who understands this critical issue is paying attention to cash levels every single day! You can "trust" this to an advisor or outsider but, especially in early times, you need to discipline yourself to be on top of these numbers. Only you can make immediate decisions as a result of what you're learning.

A combination budget and cash flow template will help you to increase your insights into your business's cash flow months into the future. Budgets are fixed, but money is not. That is, you can move money around once you understand what your reality and needs are.

The value to you is that the template gives you lead time to take action if necessary. For example, your template might show that you may have a cash shortfall three months from today. That gives you three months to plan a way to avoid the cash shortfall. That's like filling the car with fuel before the long trip, rather than desperately seeking fuel when it says "empty" and you're on a lonely stretch of road.

> **FISCAL FINESSE**
>
> *Never confuse "budget" with "money." The former is a plan for future income and spending, but the latter is a resource you can move around as needed. The needs for money trump the integrity of maintaining budgets.*

YOUR ABILITY TO RETAIN A PORTION OF YOUR EARNINGS IN YOUR BUSINESS WILL HELP YOU REDUCE YOUR CASH CYCLE

Maintaining satisfactory cash levels will be a chore in the early years of your business. That shouldn't surprise anyone. After all, here's your position:

- Insufficient brand and reputation to attract a large volume of customers
- More expenses than income for a varying period
- Unforeseen expenses arising
- Anticipated sales not occurring, or not occurring fast enough
- A few poor decisions on your learning curve.

So the manner in which you *allocate* and save some of your money as it does develop is important, because you'll be able to reduce your cash cycle and be in a stronger position in the short term.

With all of the various demands on cash (including you), it will be a delicate balancing act. There is a tendency *not* to pay certain bills, and *not* to pursue overdue fees because of an unwillingness to irritate a possible longer-term customer.

Here's a basic example: Try not to distribute 100 percent of the earnings of your business to yourself. Retaining a portion of the earnings is a big key to helping increase cash levels in your business. This takes some discipline and, perhaps, counterintuitive actions, but it pays off in a major way.

FISCAL FINESSE

Pay yourself first. Take 10 percent or 20 percent over every payment received and put it aside, in a separate account, not your business checking account.

With cash on hand in a decent amount at any given time, you're a better credit risk, and you have an emergency fund in the worst case. In the best case, you're building worth in your business and confidence in yourself. It's one thing to worry about how to raise money to meet the payroll or pay the rent, but it's quite another to know that "there's money in the bank."

With proper oversight and responsible decision-making on your part, you should be able to build up a satisfactory level of cash in your business over time. And you should be correctly asking right now, "What constitutes 'proper oversight and responsible decision-making'?"

Here are some guidelines.

- Diligently pursue overdue bills. Talk only to your customer/buyer, not someone's accounts payable department if it's a corporate sale. If you don't make efforts to do this as soon as a bill is overdue, you're enabling late payment well into the future. Otherwise, you've become someone's bank, loaning them money.
- Use methods we've already discussed here to be paid in advance with minimum or negative total days to cash. *Always* present this option if the circumstances are right.
- Delay non-mandatory expenses. In fact, don't incur them at all! This would include non-customer-facing items like office furniture, and non-urgent items like newer technology (when your current technology is serving you just fine).
- Invest the money you collect wisely. Put it in the bank despite low interest. Don't invest it in stocks or even in certificates of deposit (CDs) with a penalty if you might need the money and may have to make an early withdrawal.

Eventually, you want to be able to stop worrying about making the next payroll or paying your rent on time, because it will make your stress level unbearable. That means that, similar to the six months of expenses I advised saving for the venture at the startup point, you create a rolling six months (or more) of cash to have in reserve, perhaps building it to a year if you don't have to draw down on it.

You'll find this habit easy to perpetuate once you successfully start it and see the cash accumulate. We're not advising to resist investing in your business—this kind of cash reserve IS an investment in your business—but rather to treat "paying yourself" as a priority.

Don't let the reserves "burn a hole in your pocket." Leave them there unless urgently needed to avoid going into debt or missing a payroll. Remember our earlier discussion about people and organizations being strongest in turbulent times when they have cash.

A WORD TO THE WISE: IF YOU'RE FORTUNATE ENOUGH TO QUALIFY FOR A BUSINESS LINE OF CREDIT, BE CAREFUL HOW YOU USE IT—IT CAN BE A GIFT OR A CURSE

Be careful when you borrow funds from your business line of credit. A short-term business line of credit is supposed to be used to finance short-term assets.

A great many people have large mortgage balances today, even after 20 years or more of house ownership, because they've used a credit line attached to the home (a virtual second mortgage) for short-term needs (e.g., college tuition and an uninsured medical procedure) that was intended to be repaid but simply never was because the incremental monthly additional payment was not seen as troubling.

This thinking reduces the equity one has in a home and also deleteriously affects cash flow and credit scores. A thousand pin-pricks can be as bad as a rock falling on your head. The same dynamic applies to your business.

So we repeat: If you see the need for short-term debt for a sound business reason, then determine what cash flow expectations or enhancements will occur to repay it in the short term. Otherwise, your debt simply continues to accumulate, as do the interest payments, and your flexibility is continually reduced.

For example, you should not use your short-term business line of credit to buy long-term assets such as computers, desks, table, chairs, boats, or cars. For any "capital expense," build a budget (or build this into a budget) and seek to earn the funds. These shouldn't be impulse purchases, but rather planned acquisitions to build the business.

FISCAL FINESSE

Practice "make not take." In other words, should you encounter an unexpected need requiring funds, don't default to how to withdraw or borrow money. Instead, first ask, "How can I generate (make) more money to cover this expense?

The more you repay short-term credit lines, the more available they'll be, the more you'll be able to increase them, and the better your credit score (improving your future borrowing ability and even interest rates). But if you develop the habit of using short-term credit lines for large purchases, you'll find just the opposite: endless installments, no further credit until you repay them, and a decline in your credit score.

So, you may well be asking, "What is short-term credit for?"

You should use your short-term business line of credit to finance short-term assets, such as your accounts receivable and inventory. You'll collect those accounts receivables pretty soon (if you're disciplined and assertive), and your inventory should turn through aggressive sales efforts and marketing. You have to be thinking 90 days and not two years! (If an important computer broke down and had to be replaced, then you can draw on the "pay yourself first" funds we discussed earlier instead of using debt.) You can use it if a payroll glitch will delay salaries by a week, knowing you'll be reimbursed in a week, and thereby not causing employees hardship with a delayed check. You can use it to earn a discount (say, in airfare) that you've budgeted to spend in two weeks because you're actually saving money.

The fundamental reasoning is that your short-term assets, such as your accounts receivable and inventory, will eventually convert to cash. Your long-term assets will not! So you'll have the cash to pay back the short-term debt you undertake, but the computers and office furniture won't be paying back short-term debt over either the shorter or longer term.

When your business needs cash and you have a business line of credit, it's easy to borrow from it. Make sure you're borrowing for the right purpose or it could hurt you financially. It's a good idea to develop a relationship with a commercial banker who can advise you on the best sources of short-term cash, given your needs at the moment.

This is the difference between mediocre management and excellent management skills...and long-term survival.

NOTE

1 This may not have to be stated, but we'll include it just in case: Make sure your accounts are Federal Deposit Insurance Corporation (FDIC) insured up to the (current) maximum of $250,000 and take advantage of the fact that the limit applies to *each* account with a different EIN (Employer Identification Number). Please check with your bank for further explanation.

7

The Five Methods to Enhance Your Value While You Grow Your Business

DO YOU KNOW WHAT YOUR VALUE IS TO YOUR CLIENT?

You have to be able to quantify your value to every client in order to maximize business growth. Can you do that at the moment? Determine the value you provide to your customers and then make sure to charge appropriately for it.

Your customers might be doing this conscientiously to justify return on investment. Or they may be doing it casually and with "guesstimates." You must solidify this in order to grow via expansion, both with that client and with referrals from the client to others.

No one raves about you by saying, "They did no harm," or "They confirmed my good feelings," or "They didn't break anything!"

Qualitative value is important, of course: less stress, more free time, less conflict, faster communications. But even with these, you can generally arrive at quantifiable results: faster communications enable us to avoid scheduling overlapping and redundant calls with clients. Saving about $7,000 a month times 30 customers comes to savings of over $2.5 million per year (which is then annualized).

Defining such value enables you to calibrate whether the client truly appreciates what you're doing, and whether you and the client are recognizing the same income growth and/or savings. This should be a frequent discussion, otherwise you can readily be taken for granted. (How much help were they? Wouldn't we have done this anyway?)

DOI: 10.4324/9781032710983-7

How do you define the value that you provide to your client? That's the first thing you need to determine as you go through the exercise of how to price your product/services.

For example, if you can show that you'll provide $100,000 in value to your client, what do you think you should charge for it? Alan Weiss favors a minimum of a 10:1 return, which in this case would be $10,000.[1] If that frightens you, then try 5:1 to begin, until you can build your courage. Most consulting firms feel their clients are happy with about 3:1. So why don't you delight them, while earning more money?

FISCAL FINESSE

Your fee "basis" isn't time, but value in professional services: Alan Weiss states that you provide a dramatic return on investment (ROI) in return for equitable compensation.

Knowing your value can be a tough question to answer and there can be wildly different answers for different industries.

A BRIEF INTERLUDE ON CHARGING FOR VALUE

Alan Weiss has been preaching the benefits of value-based fees for decades. That's because charging for a time unit in professional services is totally inappropriate. The primary reason is that it's unethical. Clients deserve a rapid resolution or improvement, yet by charging by the hour, you only make major money by taking longer to deliver the solution or innovation! Never charge by the attendee, materials, or time spent—only for the result.

We know you're thinking of exceptions, but ask what each of these is worth:

- *A successful resolution to an audit in your favor or minimizing penalties*
- *An amicable divorce*
- *An estate plan minimizing taxes and maximizing legacy wealth*
- *A house or office with wonderful light and a positive nature*
- *Better client relationships and referrals*
- *Better treatment by the media*
- *A growing, powerful brand.*[2]

With products, you need "hard" pricing, no question. However, even products these days come with (highly profitable) insurance and warranties for the purchaser. (Think of "trip insurance" in these volatile times.)

But there's another aspect. People believe they get what they pay for. A high price often denotes a product of superior quality and craftsmanship. During the pandemic, many businesses survived *by raising prices*, giving an impression of longer-lasting and more reliable product.

Understanding your value is what permits you to understand what you can charge and on what basis. People are purchasing "concierge doctor" relationships, which can cost in the low five figures and are not reimbursed by insurance, but they provide the guarantee of immediate visits, no delayed callbacks, and the comfort (and safety) of immediate attention. If that can be done in medicine, it can be done in your business.

The important thing is that you figure this out as quickly as possible and make sure to charge appropriately. If you don't, you risk leaving money on the table that you'll never be able to get back. That's money you could have used to fulfill your dreams.

DON'T UNDERPRICE YOUR PRODUCTS/SERVICES BECAUSE YOU DON'T HAVE THE CONFIDENCE TO ASK FOR YOUR VALUE

You must get comfortable "asking for your value" in the same way that you got comfortable "asking for the business." Here's an exercise:

> List things you've accomplished both personally and professionally, from informally coaching someone to working in a business, from creating a new service to volunteering for a nonprofit. Then make notes on the degree to which you improved the organization and/or the individuals. Finally, ask what resulted or will result from those improvements.
>
> Example: I helped a business owner reanalyze her costs and pricing because her business was losing money. As a result of the recommended changes, the business immediately turned profitable and its pre-tax profit increased to over $1,000,000 in one year.

Setting fees and prices is a mental exercise. You have to see yourself as providing important, pragmatic, valuable products and services to others.

You *do* have a history of providing that, but you probably haven't bothered to categorize it or examine it.

We're suggesting here that you formalize it so that you can give *yourself* the assurance that you deserve to charge well.

Confidence is that important initial step. It's a word that when put into action can make challenges seem like they just melt away. But your confidence can't be reliant on your last defeat (or victory). It has to be constant.

Your self-worth shouldn't be changing daily. It should be at a constant level providing confidence. The *efficacy* of what you can do is about your skills and talents. But the self-worth you possess means you believe you're a worthy person, win or lose. You can see this in Figure 7.1.

You don't need efficacy in all aspects of your life. Perhaps you've failed to learn how to play the piano! But you should have efficacy in your business, along with high self-worth. That's the healthy position. But we all know people, perhaps ourselves, who have efficacy and perform well, but feel they're undeserving and an "imposter" in that occupation or pursuit. Then there are the people with low efficacy but huge self-esteem, who talk a good game but who really can't deliver. Pejoratively, we often refer to them as "empty suits" or "motivational junkies."

When you have neither, then you are lost: the French term for disaffection being *anomie*. There is even a type of suicide called "anomic suicide."

So you have to believe in yourself to charge for your value. It's as simple as that.

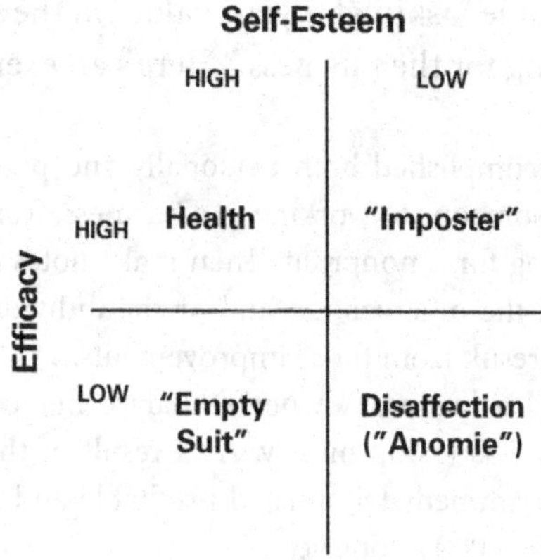

Self-Esteem

	HIGH	LOW
HIGH	Health	"Imposter"
LOW	"Empty Suit"	Disaffection ("Anomie")

(vertical axis label: Efficacy)

FIGURE 7.1

Self-esteem (worth) and efficacy. From Lifestorming, Alan Weiss and Marshall Goldsmith, John Wiley & Sons, Inc., 2017.

FISCAL FINESSE

Alan Weiss taught me, the first sale is always to yourself.

When you don't have the confidence to ask for your value, then you'll find that you'll consistently underprice your product/service. I can make a solid bet with no fear of losing, say 10:1 odds, that most business startups and entrepreneurs tend to overdeliver and undercharge. That's entirely internal and can be fatal.

If you talk to professional speakers, they'll tell you at the outset of their careers they were constantly afraid that someone would pull them off the stage saying, "You're not good enough!" (In the days of vaudeville, the emcee actually had a giant hook to pull acts off the stage if the audience started booing.)

All those stores where you see their first dollar from their first sale framed and hung on the wall have owners who were overwhelmed to get that first sale. The trouble is, they're still overwhelmed today when someone buys from them!

You're receiving compensation in return for value. That's all there is to it. Hence, if you don't have confidence in your value, your compensation—whether for a product or service—will be insufficient. When someone says, "She was a steal!" or "He's a huge bargain!" that's not good! That's a serious sign that you've underpriced. And if you think that those kinds of accolades are comforting and worth it by themselves, try paying your mortgage or repaying your debt with accolades.

Not legal tender.

How do you know your true worth? Ask yourself *and ask your customers and clients* why they deal with you, why they purchase from you, and why they were attracted to you. Remember, no one needs a drill, they need to make a hole. So stop trying to figure out how worthwhile your drill is and start trying to figure out how important that hole is to the customer.

My mentors and teachers in corporate banking taught me that I had to "ask for the business" or I wouldn't be able to close a sale. By the same token, you must learn to "ask for your value" or you won't receive it.

That last point means that the equation here is dramatic return on investment for the buyer and equitable compensation for you. The word "equitable" means "fair and valid." There are, of course, strictly commodity sales which will always be based on price: a wrench, a pencil, the person who mows your lawn. Then there are impulse sales, where the price is less a factor than the realization of an immediate need (which is why these items are often placed adjacent to the cashier): lip balm, windshield de-icer, and work gloves.

Finally, we have value purchases which are often ego-driven and emotional: autos, clothing, and televisions.[3] The farther you move up this chain, the more perceived value will determine price. This is why the iPhone outsells its closest competitors by so much in the United States (57 percent market share to runner-up Samsung's 20 percent at the end of 2022). No one requires a Rolls-Royce for transportation, but the company sells out every car it makes every year.

So creating value in the eyes of the customer ("asking for it") creates higher prices and fees. And that can include what you may think of as "commodities." Some lightbulbs demonstrate longer life than others. Some refrigerators are "smart," as are some washers and dryers. Some lawn care firms will aerate and overseed besides just cutting the grass.

The firm that removes the dog waste from our yard twice a week can charge whatever they like as far as I'm concerned.

Some of you may get comfortable asking for value right away. For others, like me, it took time to get comfortable asking for my value. Don't give up. Keep pushing yourself. Once you get comfortable asking for your value, it changes everything for you in a positive way. There is no going back.

People believe they get what they pay for. They tend to "like" a theatrical event much more when they've paid a great deal of money for seats, irrespective of the actual artistic worth. We rave about vacations that cost a lot, and favor clothing that's expensive, even if it's not as attractive on us as less expensive items.

During the pandemic, as we've noted, many firms stayed in business and improved their financial condition *by raising prices*. And remember that providing services remotely, and products through the web and/or mail order, should not lessen their price because the value is in the eyer of the purchaser.

A great many small business owners thought the pandemic killed their businesses. But it was they who killed their own businesses in the frantic doom-loop of trying to lower prices to attract buyers, instead of raising prices to attract buyers. It sounds counterintuitive, but it's absolutely true. You don't make up losses on volume!

AS YOU MAKE SALES TO SIMILAR SIZE COMPANIES, START BUILDING YOUR CONFIDENCE AND THEN DEDICATE A PORTION OF YOUR SALES AND MARKETING EFFORTS TO LARGER COMPANIES

Larger companies have larger budgets.

Period.

As you start to grow your business, start developing a plan to go up-market. This means that as you get better at being in tune with your customers' wants and needs, start prospecting for larger companies. Closing larger sales to larger companies will not only make you more profits, it will also give you a boost in confidence.

That sounds easier said than done. But consider these sources of referral to larger customers:

- Existing customers' suppliers
- Existing customers' customers [if they are business-to-business (B-2B)]
- Local chambers of commerce
- Local service clubs (e.g., Rotary)
- Private clubs that often host outsiders in their "enrichment series"
- Professional resources (doctors, attorneys, dentists, designers, etc.)
- Items about businesses in local and regional publications.

If you allot time to pursuing these sources of connection with larger prospects, you'll be successful. But this assumes you're running your own business efficiently and with managed, profitable growth so that you have the time to pursue larger businesses instead of "fighting your own fires."

It will also help you to learn how larger companies do business, and it may help you to shed the small business mentality you had when you started. Some distinctions of larger organizations for you to consider (check off the ones you have experienced):

___ Often use requests for proposals (RFPs) for larger purchases

___ Often have buyers who are not the CEO or founder

___ Sometimes have varied locations with independent buying

___ Can demand appearance on an "approved vendor" list

___ Demand you go through "procurement" or "purchasing"

___ Over-focus on price as compared to value
___ Delay payments or have restrictive payment terms
___ Sometimes *must* accept discounts for payment in full at the outset
___ Have a huge potential for referral business.

Some of these are drawbacks, but some are clearly opportunities. If you haven't checked many of them, you need to do your homework to prepare yourself for a different kind of marketing, sale, and relationship.

Bear in mind that a single $100,000 sale *is far more profitable than ten $10,000 sales even though the revenues are the same.* That's one of the very significant benefits of pursuing larger prospects in larger markets. The scalability and leverage are significant.

FISCAL FINESSE

No small business should seek to stay small. Growth is critical to survival and innovation is critical to growth.

Depending on the nature of your business, you may discover that in some cases, you are putting a similar amount of time and effort into a larger sale as you do a smaller sale.

Here's an exercise that we recommend even our veteran clients (and readers) utilize: Keep a time log over two weeks of your activities *specifically with clients.* This can include:

- Marketing
- Sales
- Service
- Research and design
- Customized products and services
- Pricing
- Referral requests and follow-up.

Be specific as to which clients are receiving your cumulative time once you add all this up. Some activities (such as research and design) might be spread over several or all clients. But most will be specific.

Then do the same thing for *prospects.*

Now, ask yourself which clients are bringing you the most profit (not revenues) and which prospects *are likely to bring you the most profits.*

Too many businesses spend 70 percent of their time focused on 15 percent of their revenues. We are not making this up. When you respond to the "squeaky wheel" of a poor client with low profitability, that's what's happening.

Make sure that most of your time is applied to your most profitable clients and prospects. That's where the high ROI exists.

From a math perspective, it takes a smaller amount of larger sales to meet your growth goals.

Also from a time management perspective, that rule is absolute. New business acquisition is far more expensive—in terms of both time and money—than expansion business with existing customers. Hence, it makes sense to try to reduce the expenses associated with new business sales: marketing, sales, promotional collateral, tests, pilots, returns, multiple meetings for one sale, and so forth. As we've noted previously, it takes the same amount of blood, sweat, and tears to close a $100,000 customer as a $10,000 customer, or a $1,000 customer as a $500 one.

And if you think back to our exercise on the time log and where you're spending your time vis-à-vis prospects, then ask yourself if that time is spent on larger and larger customers providing higher levels of profit, or small customers providing minimal levels of profit.

Think of the lifetime value of the client. Will this prospect likely develop into a long-term, valued client who provides significant referrals, larger and larger purchases, and very few complaints or returns? If so, they are worth "romancing" and spending time developing. The initial sale may be somewhat small, but what will the cumulation be over the years?

DEVELOP WAYS TO INCREASE THE VALUE OF YOUR EXISTING PRODUCTS/SERVICES TO YOUR CUSTOMERS

As you grow your business, you should focus on creating more value for your customers. More value will translate into more profits. As you can see in Figure 7.2, most customers know what they want, *but they don't always realize what they need.* Pointing out that difference is the "value distance."[4] The greater that distance, the more you can charge.

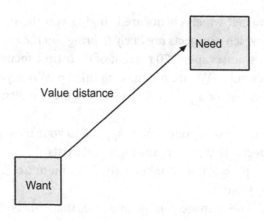

FIGURE 7.2
Need versus want.

What people "want" is usually a commodity subject to price competition: an airline seat, a refrigerator, their taxes completed, and so forth. But when you introduce an unforeseen *need*, there is no longer price competition because the offer is now one of uniqueness. An airline ticket to Paris is one thing, but what is a curated, private tour of the Louvre worth? A pool pump and heater is one thing, but what if you could control them anywhere in the world from your smartphone?

Your existing customers will tell you what they like and dislike about your products and services, which will help you determine how to increase the value, but more importantly, how to make them singular and non-commodities. Coaching is a highly competitive service, but it's rather unique when you bring together a small group of similar executives who otherwise would never have met, because one of them suggests he or she would love to meet kindred spirits.

The same product/service can have a completely different value to another customer. Speaking of coaching, you may use the exact same methodology with a front-line supervisor as with a division vice president, but because the latter has so much more impact and financial responsibility, that coaching becomes unique and higher priced. (Most "life coaches" today make relatively little money because they don't differentiate themselves and the title has become generic.)

Your mission is to find other areas where your products and services can command higher value. As you can see, it's not that difficult if you refuse to settle for the "same old, same old," and don't just respond to what the customer "wants."

FISCAL FINESSE

When someone tells you what they want, ask "Why do you want that?" and you'll find a higher-level need that's unexpressed.

CREATE NEW, HIGHER-VALUE PRODUCTS AND SERVICES

Your existing customers are in the best position to tell you what additional needs they have and what else they would likely buy from you if you created it. All you need to do is ask them. *However*, they are likely to tell you what they need today, or even what they needed yesterday.

You need to find out what they will probably need tomorrow!

So don't simply ask what they need, ask what they think they'll probably need in the near future given:

- Competition
- New markets being considered
- The likely economy
- Social mores
- Technology
- Demographics.

Around 2030, there will be more people over 65 in the United States than there will be children, which is unprecedented. (In Japan, it's going to be more severe than that.) What does that mean for your customers' customers?

If you don't think that's an important issue, consider this: In the United States, a very hot TV show has been *The Bachelor*, in which a young, good-looking guy selects a wife from an assortment of young, good-looking women. Now, they've launched *The Golden Bachelor*, who's 72 and his female candidates range in age from the late 50s to late 70s. That's because streaming services are stealing away younger viewers, so the traditional broadcast channels are focusing on their "tried and true" older audiences.

You could simply ask them what other "hot button" issues they have at the present time. That will provide you with a starting point for a conversation and then extend it into the immediate future. Take it from there and start asking questions and you never know where the conversation will lead. That's because your customers don't often have these conversations!

During the Great Recession, I developed a new, higher-value service for my clients which I named "Bank Relations." It happened because I asked! I asked a client if there was anything else I could do to help them, and they told me that they wished there was a way they could learn how to talk to their bank. Since I successfully passed through a commercial bank's formal training program and went on to work as a corporate banker, I knew that I could help the client successfully.

Then, I asked the rest of my clients if they found value in learning how to talk to their bank. They said yes. The next step was a page on my website dedicated to "Bank Relations," and I always mentioned this capability during prospect meetings. My new, value-added service was right in front of my face and I had no clue until I asked.

Keep in mind that even if you have a trusting relationship with your clients, they might not be willing to share certain business-related matters with you because sometimes they're embarrassed! Don't take it personally.

Some businesses simply send a letter. Personally, I am not a big fan of that approach, but I understand why they do it. In my opinion, it's such a difficult topic that they don't want to address it face-to-face with the client. Therefore, they write a letter instead of having a conversation. This approach might work for some people, but for those of us with aspirations to be our clients' trusted advisor, we need a more personal approach. That brings us to the first secret.

THE SIX SECRETS TO SUCCESSFUL PRICE INCREASES

- **#1: Don't beat around the bush about a price increase**. Own it and be up-front about it. The first few times may be uncomfortable, but eventually, you'll feel comfortable doing it. Your client will appreciate your honesty. Add value in order to raise prices.
- **#2: If you still can't get comfortable talking to your existing clients about a price increase, then only raise prices for your new clients**. This approach helps you to become mentally prepared for the conversation and can take the pressure off of you. Remember, you have to do what works for you!

- **#3: Insert an annual price increase sentence into your engagement letter and/or contract**. That way, there's plenty of advance notice for your client. When the time comes for the price increase, well, you have already had this conversation with your client at the beginning of the relationship. Now, it is simply a matter of reminding them politely.
- **#4: Be keenly aware of the timing of your price increase**. A proposed price increase to a client that is not happy with your product/service will not be successful.
- **#5: Never make your clients feel that they are getting less from you as you are increasing your price**. A successful price increase should make your customers feel that the value they're receiving from you is better than it was before the price increase. If you can make the client feel that you've added value along with the price increase, that's an even better outcome.
- **#6: Never sit down at the negotiating table unless you're willing to get up and walk away empty-handed**. This means that there's a risk you might not have a successful price increase and you may lose this client. Therefore, weigh your options carefully.

NOTES

1 For details on value-based pricing, see *Value Based Fees*, Alan Weiss, John Wiley, 2021.
2 Ibid.
3 A car is the largest "lifestyle" purchase that most people make on a regular basis.
4 Weiss, *Value-Based Fees*.

8

Using Technology to Reduce Costs and Boost Your Productivity

The advent of technology has brought with it great increases in productivity. As this is written, new vistas await with developments such as telehealth, artificial intelligence (AI), same-day delivery of online purchases, and even advanced Uber scheduling!

Technology for its own sake, however, is never a sufficient reason. It's like creating an electric fork. The ability is there, but the application isn't. On the other hand, putting small "tags" to put in your airline luggage to track their location—or on your dog's collar—is a great idea.

When is a technological intervention potentially "great"?

- It's easy to build or acquire.
- It adds value to our products and services.
- Customers are willing to pay more for that value.
- It's easy to implement and requires little or no servicing.
- It's pragmatic and immediately applicable.

Technological innovation can also be a disaster. Think of all those automated checkout lanes in stores where customers curse and yell, and store personnel have to help them through the technology that was introduced to replace them! Don't you love the repetitive, automated, cold voice stating, "Place your items in the bagging area. Please place your items in the bagging area..."

These increases in productivity have led to reductions in costs. You'll find both internal and external cost savings, if you apply technology correctly (and *not* for its own sake). You can take an innovative approach to improve your business. For example, auto dealerships make most of their profit from

DOI: 10.4324/9781032710983-8

service, not sales. The "OnStar" service on many cars provides a monthly diagnostic of the oil life, tire pressure, warranty status, and so forth. A green sign means all is well, amber means that some steps need to be taken to prevent problems, and red means get yourself to the dealer ASAP.

Consequently, instead of set and often arbitrary service intervals, the consumer can take action to see the dealer with legitimate maintenance needs that might otherwise go unnoticed (when was the last time you checked your tire pressure or oil levels?), thereby improving safety and the dealer's business.

Many of us are attracted to hotels which, while otherwise in very competitive marketplaces, offer us advance check-in on their apps and keyless access to our rooms, bypassing the front desk lines entirely. An increasing number of travelers use Global Entry and a quick retinal scan as an express route through immigration and customs, and use a phone app to speed through Transportation Security Administration (TSA) processing.

There are "cashless" stores where your credit card is charged when you remove something from a shelf (think of hotel minibars which do this), so that both human and automated cashiers are eliminated.

You may be able to reduce costs internally by using technology to automate certain tasks that were historically done manually. We hear about the elusive "digital transformation" all the time, which is hard to comprehend. But pragmatically, it means exactly this: changing laborious and expensive manual tasks to automated and efficient low-cost ones. One example most of us encounter regularly is the automated "chat" on many service sites. Before you're connected to a "live" agent, you're asked a series of questions by a "bot" which has helpful suggestions. (And sometimes there is no option for a human agent.)

We visited a prosciutto (Italian ham) plant, one of the two largest in the country. The meat has to be cured and stored at varying temperatures and humidity over many months. This was once the essence of physical labor. However, now, small robots automatically move stacks of 70 sides of beef from one storage area to another, including through otherwise closed doors which are opened for them. More sophisticated robots actually cut the meat when it's ready to be packaged.

Only the highly customized and special cutting is done by humans.

If this can happen in the processing of meat, it can certainly happen in any kind of organization. You need to be receptive to these kinds of "transformational" ideas.

FISCAL FINESSE

Technology for technology's sake is like driving for driving's sake. You burn fuel and put wear on the car, but you don't arrive anywhere important.

On the external side, review your business to determine where you could use technology to reduce costs without negatively impacting your customers' experience.

Perhaps you've experienced this unpleasantness: Hotels that once replaced the partially used shampoos, conditioners, and liquid soaps daily now depend on the maids to replace them only if they're empty. This is cost-cutting, but on a self-defeating basis; since the maids often forget, the guests are unhappy and have to request replacements, and it all winds up costing more time and labor than before.

We've noted that it makes no sense to have automated cashier stations if you have to position the same number of employees to help customers use them.

However, good examples also abound. ATMs are effective and save bank staffing. They've become ubiquitous in hotel lobbies, casinos, shopping malls, and even convenience stores.

The key is to use technology to reduce expenses where there are only small possibilities of adverse consequences.

You can be better organized, more productive, and for less money. But you don't do this by jumping on every fad, backing up your systems 15 times, and creating elaborate and complicated websites. You do this by:

- Asking yourself what you find advantageous using technology from other firms. For example, being able to schedule an Uber in advance is often a lifesaver. Why can't customers order products in advance to be picked up at designated times (like your pharmacy schedules flu shots online)?
- Asking your customers for their ideas. You can do this in a newsletter, or suggestion box, or even in your bills! What do they think can be speeded up, or made more convenient, from what they've experienced elsewhere?

- Read the business news. Find out what innovations people are talking about. Do you need to accept Apple Card payments, or Venmo, or PayPal? Should you be using texts instead of emails? What about Instagram?

Technology *wisely used* can save you money and make you a fortune.

WEB CONFERENCING

This technology started in the 1990s. It might end up being one of the most impactful boosters of productivity in our lifetimes.

Web conferencing may have been popularized with Webex and Skype, but now people "Zoom" everything.

This is, by the way, an example of how one technological approach can sweep out another. No one Skypes anymore, to the extent that it's odd to hear it. You tend to stream today and not change channels or "surf." When you see "AOL" after an internet address, you're prone to be amazed AOL is still in business, right?

Zoom and other remote options (e.g., Google Meet) were popular pre-pandemic, but became the default mechanism when people couldn't travel. And, like take-out food even at high-end restaurants, it has become a fixture of post-pandemic society and business. This is because:

- It's relatively cheap and often free (someone else's Zoom);
- The quality is high (although interruptions occur, depending on the network quality);
- You can join by phone, tablet, or computer, with or without a camera switched on;
- It operates well internationally;
- It is available in all time zones 24/7;
- Recording is immediate and painless and records are created;
- One can attend in real time or watch the replay;
- Without the need for travel, meetings are far less costly and disruptive;

- Live meetings can be conducted from anywhere; instead of a phone call, you can see your client's face in a quick web meeting: that helps to solidify business relationships and saves money at the same time;
- It enables you to reach more clients, which leads to growth in business revenues.

Web conferencing is totally acceptable in business these days. If you're fearful about using it, then pick one client and try it. Or try it with a social group, civic group, or bunch of buddies. Don't get involved in all the "bells and whistles," just get comfortable. People make the mistake of thinking they have to master all aspects. I use about 20 percent of the full power of my computer, but I use 100 percent of that 20 percent.

FISCAL FINESSE

Be prudent and pragmatic. There are features on our cars that most of us don't ever use for as long as we drive the vehicle!

ACCOUNTING SOFTWARE

Accounting used to be done by hand. Think volumes of paper, pencils, and erasers as well as walls of file cabinets. When I graduated from college in 1987, a typical accounting department consisted of many accounting employees using typewriters (ahem, personal computers in business were still very expensive infants) and sitting in a massive office space.

For business owners, accounting was a painful exercise due to its labor-intensive nature. Real-time information? Forget about it! You would be making today's business decisions based on financial information that was months old.

Yet we duplicate some of these ineffective practices today. We attempt to do our own books, our own payroll, even our own taxes (sales, property, state, federal, and so forth) instead of investing (yes, *investing*) in outside expertise to do it faster and better, and avoid the demands on our own precious time.

How about the safety of your accounting information? Do you want sensitive financial information sitting in file cabinets all over your office?

If you accept credit and debit cards in your business, you're obligated to conform to certain security controls by your provider and/or bank. These have to be scrupulously maintained, not just to continue your processing privileges but also to avoid consumer lawsuits from hacking and information leaks.

FISCAL FINESSE

Ignoring the benefits of state-of-the-art accounting software and external expertise is like trying to repair your own television. Not only will you not get a clear picture, but you're also likely to hurt yourself!

Consider location: Before accounting software, you would have to go where your accounting information was located in order to review it. Now, you can review this information anywhere you have an internet connection. You can save it more easily and convey it (to accountants, attorneys, board members, and so forth) more easily.

Using accounting software saves you money because you can get everything you need to make timely business decisions at your fingertips. No more huge file cabinets in costly office space.

Have you visited a doctor or dentist and found that they still maintain huge paper files in large cabinets because they've refused to transfer them digitally ("digital transformation")? These are subject to loss, misfiling, and worse: HIPAA[1] violations occur when sensitive data is left on a countertop for others to see.

Accounting software is the safest way to maintain privacy, avoid careless errors, and ensure customer and client confidentiality. It's true that systems can be hacked, but there are security systems available to make that a less likely possibility.

EMAIL SOFTWARE

Due to its now indispensable value in life, many of us have forgotten how much money email software saves your business. From the massive reduction in paper printing costs to the massive reduction in postage costs, email software continues to be a huge cost-saver for business.

Not only does email software reduce costs, it also speeds up our communication which results in even more cost savings.

This isn't a technology book, but a few pragmatic business points about email are helpful.

- Have a separate business and personal address. Not only does this separate correspondence, but it also provides a backup should one fail to work, which does happen, unfortunately.
- Don't use email as a storage system. Create files and folders for your clients, suppliers, employees, R&D, sales—whatever. Your daily email should be either deleted after a response (if a response is needed), filed in the appropriate folder, or printed out if a paper copy is needed (i.e., to have your signature notarized).
- At a normal day's end, your physical desk AND your electronic desk should be empty and clean.

FISCAL FINESSE

Return to hard copy, handwritten notes for special occasions of emphasis: thank you, congratulations, condolences, special events, and so forth.

I am mentioning email because your own email list will prove to be one of your most valuable business assets and the marketing gold for business. You can no longer depend on social media networks because their algorithms are constantly changing and dramatically reducing your exposure to your "followers." (Plus, they are full of disinformation and misinformation.)

You own your email list and, therefore, are in control of how you utilize it for distribution. No one can take it away from you, although carelessness and poor security can remove it or compromise it. But with its intelligent use, you're not subject to the whims of *someone else's* business model.

CUSTOMER RELATIONSHIP MANAGEMENT TOOLS

Using a Customer Relationship Management (CRM) tool ties together your lead generation, sales, customer service, and marketing. These can begin as modest trackers—simple spreadsheets and tracking programs—and evolve into sophisticated follow-up and marketing tools. My advice is to start simple. If you're buying your first car, you probably don't want a Ferrari—even if you can afford it—because you're not going to be able to handle it without a lot of driving experience.

Start small and relatively inexpensively.

The primary rationale for CRM tools is that it's enormously more expensive (and, hence, far lower margins) to acquire a new customer than it is to sustain and build an existing one. Moreover, "customer relationship" should also include "prospective customer relationship," because you can save enormous amounts of money and time by collapsing the sales cycle for new business acquisition as well.

When you begin your business, you may track your prospect follow-up by using a calendar on your phone and tablet, or even with a paper calendar and diary such as a Filofax®. (Don't laugh, paper diaries don't "crash" and they're seldom left behind anywhere or stolen.) At a gym I attend, the owner keeps track of customers and training regimens on a huge whiteboard on the wall. This isn't sophisticated, but it works for him.

I'm not suggesting Etch-A-Sketch (yes, it's still produced!), but simply advising that you don't need the most comprehensive option to begin.

No matter what option you choose, CRM tools should make it easy for you to:

- Know the dates that you contacted a client/prospect and what you discussed with them;
- Know what you emailed to them and when;
- Know what you sold them and when;
- Know key facts about them (and perhaps their families and/or workers) including anniversaries, birthdays, business milestones, and so forth);
- Keep track of all incoming and outgoing customer service matters;
- Keep track of the referrals they've provided, which resulted in business, and how much;
- Track key points of expansion and continuation business, such as service warranty renewals, servicing of the product if appropriate, new software associated with past purchases, and special deals offered by your wholesalers that can be passed on to the client;
- Keep tabs on requests that can't be fulfilled as yet (supply chain issues, later release dates, recalls).

Imagine the time savings associated with using this type of tool!

FISCAL FINESSE

Customers typically don't track even their own past requests, but they're remarkably responsive when you tell them renewals, updates, and improvements are available.

PROJECT MANAGEMENT TOOLS

Project management tools have brought order to what once was a chaotic process for managing projects. But if you have customer management tools, you might be curious about why you need project management tools.

Imagine trying to manage a project that has employees located in different physical locations. How would you keep track of the progress? Project management tools provide you with a way to centralize the project management online. Today, it's far more likely that you may have widely separated employees, subcontractors, and suppliers. They may well be in different time zones. Even if you chose to phone them, you couldn't reasonably do so, and your email would probably require 12–24 hours for a decent response.

Project management allows you to:

- Assign tasks and outcomes with timelines
- Provide and receive reports of all team members' progress
- Alert everyone about unexpected delays or advantages
- Ask for inputs and advice on challenges that arise in others' areas
- Effectively track time and monetary investments and make intelligent reallocations when needed.

FISCAL FINESSE

A project has many "moving parts." They can be tightly managed and controlled, or they can manage and control you.

No two projects are alike, so your software has to allow for distinctions from situation to situation. There is no "one size fits all."

Suppose you're creating a new software solution for customer orders that accommodates credit cards, third parties such as PayPal and Venmo, existing credits, and returns, you can:

- Create a project with a customized timeline;
- Assign different roles and responsibilities to each member of the project;
- Track your project expenses inside the project;
- Keep your client apprised of progress (even daily), which is a common and sometimes fatal mistake when not done;
- Track "beta testing" and pilot tests;
- Reward those people who finish ahead of schedule and under budget;
- Appreciate who is best to place on various projects and against what needs.

This type of tool helps to keep you and your team better organized, which leads to less time wasted and more projects brought in on budget.

ARTIFICIAL INTELLIGENCE TOOLS

Artificial intelligence (AI) tools are presently in their infancy and learning rapidly. These are tools *which should make your life easier—not more difficult, produce quality work—not failure work, and reduce expenses—not increase them.*

AI often provides very simple, rapid solutions: answering "frequently asked questions," providing automated responses to generic questions, correcting entry errors (or requesting that they be corrected in real time), confirming appointments, producing diagnostic reports, creating common contracts, generating clear instructions and illustrations, and responding to both written and oral inquiries.

Earlier, we mentioned such advantages as keyless access to hotel rooms, remote starting of cars and equipment, reminders about everything from medicine to reorder, and preparations for meetings and appointments.

The key questions for you to answer about whether to purchase and deploy AI are:

- Will this meet a legitimate and frequent customer need in a high-quality manner?
- Is this a situation where human contact and empathy are *not* required?
- Will this avoid frustration and further unhappiness on the part of the user?
- Does it provide a human "backup" in case of trouble? (Don't think that customers believe that calls are actually monitored for "training purposes" when the actual performance never improves!)

Restaurant servers, police officers, and manicurists all use AI. Shoemakers, carpenters, and therapists probably do not (although I stand to be corrected). People will sit and tell their woes to a bartender they don't know well, but probably not to a robotic drink dispenser. I don't believe a therapist using a tablet will be seen as more thoughtful than one with a pad and pencil.

It's too early to tell where these tools will make their biggest mark, but the early results are interesting. AI tools are popular right now for their extensive content-creation skills. Ask the AI tool to write you a blog and it can do a pretty fine job!

FISCAL FINESSE

Whenever personality, mood, and/or empathy are required, don't resort to AI. Use your own emotions and words. Otherwise, what's supposed to be personal will sound generic.

It's not just the content we're discussing. AI tools have *answers to many questions* they're being asked right now. The tools work 24/7. They don't require rest. They're constantly updated. On the surface, AI tools seem like they may boost productivity more than all of the technology tools discussed above—combined.

But we all know that spelling checkers on our phones and tablets often create more errors than they correct. We know that we still have to "unplug and plug back in" when we have inexplicable technology issues with equipment and software. And while I've never seen an ATM that produces more money than asked, I have seen them swallow a card and not return it, having granted no money at all.

Autonomous cars are still hitting things. Don't allow AI to smack you.

NOTE

1 Health Insurance Portability and Accountability Act.

9

Valuation Is Now

PREPARATION IS KEY TO MAXIMIZING VALUE BECAUSE VALUATION SURPRISES ARE A ROAD OVER A CLIFF

As an entrepreneur, one of the toughest decisions to make is when to sell your business and for how much. Surprisingly, a vast number of owners don't consider preparing for this until they're ready to sell! Even if the sale is forced by illness or disruption, there is no excuse for not having your business in the best possible shape to be attractive to potential buyers.

In the next chapter, we'll talk about one's legacy and the fact that your legacy is being created *every day*. Similarly, the worth of your business—its valuation—is created every day. You don't simply put a "for sale" sign outside your home if you choose to sell it without first making it maximally attractive to your identified prospective buyers.

The same holds true for your business.

FISCAL FINESSE

Focusing on improving valuation every day also increases your profitability every day, so the short-term benefits are as important as the eventual benefits in a sale price.

Selling your business requires the same amount of discipline that you used in order to grow your business. Picture a house that's "staged" by an expert realtor prior to being shown to prospective buyers. There's no subterfuge—certain rooms aren't blocked off—but the place is cleaned up,

                              DOI: 10.4324/9781032710983-9

perhaps painted, the landscaping is tended to, furniture and lighting may be rearranged, and so on.

With your business, you can't pretend you have more business than you do (there are laws against that!), but you can show there are no overdue receivables, expenses have been reduced or profits increased, staffing is stable, promotion is ongoing, and the brand is attracting leads. But you can't create that overnight any more than you can create a new look for your house overnight.

Hence, it's a good idea to seek a broker who is an expert in these kinds of sales when the time is right. But well before that, perhaps years before, *perhaps a generation before*, you need to consider how to keep your business optimally performing, demonstrating controlled and profitable growth, and fixing any problems (such as out-of-date equipment, poor software, unfilled positions, and dated marketing collateral).

Remember that the preparation for a high valuation of your business *also means greater profits in the short run*. It's far easier to do this gradually and consistently than trying to do it rapidly in the hopes of a quick sale. You want to be seen as a well-run, progressive business all the time, not just "in the end of times."

In order to put yourself in the best position to maximize the sale of your business, you must make sure that you're properly prepared. This preparation is referred to as an "exit strategy." There are consultants and coaches who specialize solely in this need. And, believe it or not, this is a concern even among huge businesses that were founded and run by families. Quite some time ago, there were ugly lawsuits among the family members of the Pritzker family (of Hyatt Hotel fame).

Some considerations that can be short term or very long term:

- Owners' compensation
- Employee numbers and stability
- Trademarks, copyrights, and patents
- Receivables
- Debt and credit rating
- Customer stability and "churn"
- Profit per sale and per customer
- Physical plant and facilities
- Software and technology status and modernization.

Preparation for a successful sale that meets your desired outcome will take a considerable amount of your time. Keep in mind that you'll still be running your business during this time period. Therefore, you'll have added an extra "hat" to your existing responsibilities (the "hats" we described earlier)—one that will make you extremely busy as well as emotionally invested.

In effect, you're dealing with the present and the future of your business at once! The idea is to be synergistic. Don't simply "understand," but behave in a manner that demonstrates that your current actions will create a bright future and that bright future is the reason for your current actions (and sacrifices, requirements, demands, and, sometimes, exhaustion).

Organizations that learn from their past, align themselves with the present, and reap the rewards in the future are on a positive and self-perpetuating journey. You don't have to live like a pauper today; just not like King Midas. And you don't have to "bet big" on tomorrow, just prepare correctly for it.

As we age (both as people and as businesses), more and more expected and unexpected events transpire. These could be illness, loss of interest, family issues, outmoded technology, stronger competitors, and so on. If we learn correctly and apply our learning, we'll have wisdom, which will help us avoid much of this and be able to better deal with what we can't avoid.

START PREPARING TO INCREASE VALUE NOW FOR A SALE THAT YOU EXPECT TO CLOSE WITHIN 24–36 MONTHS

Based on best practices as determined by historical business sale experiences, a business owner should start preparing for the sale of the business at least 24–36 months prior to the anticipated sale closing date. Sooner is even better because, as we've established, in the interim, your business becomes more profitable to you in the present, not solely in the future.

It's a good idea to have an outside expert perform a forensic (methodological) examination of the operation. Many owners, constantly on the move and often "fighting fires," see only the surface and superficial levels. A decline in revenue from a key client might really be indicating that the client is leaving. Slowly increasing revenue year-to-year might mean that the enterprise is replacing lost customers with new business, but not sustaining that business beyond the short term. Three people leaving over the course of a year might actually reflect a poor middle manager driving them away.

An expert can also provide metrics to judge your success rather than merely comparing yourself to competitors (who themselves might be performing sub-par). For example, a consulting firm ought to be producing at least $250,000 in revenue per employee (or full-time equivalency in the event of part-timers and subcontractors). So, before patting yourself on the back for a great year, perhaps you need to apply some of these measures.

FISCAL FINESSE

If you prepare for a wedding, major vacation, or birth far in advance, why on earth wouldn't you do the same for the sale of your most important asset?

The 24–36-month (or longer) timeframe will provide the selling business owner with the time needed to ensure that the business is performing in a way that will justify the asking price. The longer the timeframe, the more you can accommodate dips and downturns, which will fall into perspective amid larger, overall growth. (Think of a resume, where one short-term job isn't important among several longer ones, but a series of short-term jobs is probably a "red flag.")

All enterprises suffer some setbacks over competitive actions, poor economies, technological changes, retirements, natural disasters, regulatory changes, and so forth. The key is to show that the organization has been resilient in "bouncing forward" from the setback. Think of a series of waves and troughs. You don't want to be trying to sell your company when it's in a trough.

There will be significant amounts of work to do in order to review and/or improve your company's revenue, profits, accounting, and internal procedures. These are areas which merit decent investments, which is why we've suggested external experts wherever appropriate. You don't want a potential buyer's expert to be the one pointing out areas of weakness. You want to clean these up first.

Ensure that all of your business's books and records are complete, because you'll go through a thorough due diligence process by the buyer. This will include a careful review of the investments that you're presently making in your business because your exit strategy will change everything.

This means that you need to be 100 percent focused on maximizing your revenue and profits.

For example, if you want to sell in 36 months, you should be cautious not to make investments in your business that have a 60-month payback; unless there's a compelling strategic reason. Otherwise, you might be negatively impacting your financial results. While longer-term thinking is usually a great positive, in this example, you need to confine your "longer-term" thinking to 36 months. A buyer wants to see what's in the equation upon the sale, not after the sale, and certainly not what's still conjecture.

An exception would be client contracts that run past 36 months and demonstrate continuing revenues and profits post-sale. These are "annuities" that would make sense and be attractive to a buyer, because the buyer doesn't have to "restart" the company after the actual sale is consummated. Another exception would be employee contracts which show that key people are obligated to stay and won't be departing upon the sale date, guaranteeing continuity and a constant client interface.

DO NOT OVERESTIMATE YOUR BUSINESS'S VALUATION

What is my business worth? That's a question I'm asked every month and I do my best to avoid answering!

For one thing, "worth" is in the eye of the beholder. When you try to personally sell a car, you emphasize all the great points while glossing over a few scratches and dings. The prospective buyer will focus on the cosmetic problems while conveniently ignoring the low mileage.

And, as you probably know, buying and selling houses is even worse! That's why most people use realtors who know how to stress the positives and can talk to the other party's realtor in common terms. (And it's also why most realtors will demand the sellers leave the property during an "open house" so there's no chance of hurt feelings or confrontations over prospective buyers' comments!)

Your business is also, in many ways, your "house."

FISCAL FINESSE

You need an independent third party to help you assess your business's worth, especially in volatile economic times.

There are so many variables that go into the valuation of a business that it can get complicated. There's no "one size fits all" answer. Businesses that have the same dollar amount of annual revenue and operate in completely different industries can carry vastly different valuations.

Economic times also play a direct role in the valuation of a business. In stronger economic times, values are higher, and, conversely, in weaker economic times, the values are lower. *In volatile times, valuation can vary significantly, which is why you need to build a solid, documented record of growth.*

Make sure you understand how the variables of valuation work, so that you aren't disappointed!

Example: My friend sold his information technology company with $10 million annual revenue for $50 million dollars. Well, that means that my $20 million in revenue commodity manufacturing company must be worth at least that amount, if not more. Actually, no, it doesn't.

You're asking $10 million dollars for your business: but is it really worth $10 million dollars in your field, in your market, under current conditions? Perhaps, but there's no guarantee, and my friend's experience may actually be irrelevant.

Managing your expectations in a reasonable manner will help you to meet your valuation outcome. We all tend to overestimate worth, and, in this case, it's wise to be very conservative, so we're not disappointed.

PUT YOURSELF IN YOUR BUYER'S SHOES

How will the buyer finance the acquisition of your business? Will it meet your monetary needs?

There are some buyers who can afford to pay your asking price in cash. Most buyers choose to finance a portion of the asking price in order to boost their investment return. Therefore, you can gain some critical information by putting yourself in your buyer's shoes from a financing perspective.

What if you were buying your business? What would you see as attractive and unattractive? This might be difficult to do in "removing" yourself from your intimacy with your business, and it's why it can be highly beneficial to have a broker or impartial third-party help with that assessment. (Recall our home realtor example.)

There are questions you may never have thought about asking since you started your own business (or inherited it) which someone buying a business might find important. This will vary by business type, location, customers, prospects, age of equipment, current economy, and so forth.

With high interest rates, buyers may prefer to use mostly cash. With low interest rates, financing might be more attractive. This is where your banker may be of huge help, especially if the bank is offering favorable loans for business acquisitions, or the state is offering benefits (e.g., tax incentives) to people buying or opening businesses.

Let's say your asking price for your business is $10 million and you have a service company. If your buyer wants to finance a portion of the asking price, who can provide the financing for them?

Does your business have enough tangible assets that your proposed buyer can use as collateral to get financing from a bank? If your business's assets consist of only computers, tables, and chairs, then the answer is probably no. If you feel you do have the requisite assets, does your banker agree? Or can the buyer's banker agree?

Some buyers take a partial payment and receive a leveraged buyout—the balance owed is paid out of future profits from the business. This enables the sale and is a good idea if the business is generating revenues that are growing and are solid (e.g., long-term clients). Don't forget that all of your compensation (and that of any other family members who would be leaving with the sale) becomes equity in the business, and the new buyers might well choose to take less compensation until you're paid off.

These arrangements are not uncommon, but need careful legal structure and require ideal buyers. You can't trust your future payoff balance to people who don't really understand the business, or try to take too much personal compensation, or who simply aren't good business people. Leveraged buyouts are popular, but include significantly higher risk.

I strongly advise against continuing to work in the business, even part-time, to help maintain revenue *because then you're working to pay yourself off.*

FISCAL FINESSE

Never just "settle" for a buyer. Evaluate the buyer's background and history, just as the buyer is evaluating your business. Both sides need to perform "due diligence."

If the proposed sale of your business doesn't meet the credit guidelines for a bank to provide the financing, then it will be more difficult and certainly more expensive to find financing. In that case, who would provide the financing?

There are other potential financing sources in the market, but bank financing is sometimes the cheapest. Since you're putting yourself in your proposed buyer's shoes, your challenge right now is to find a source willing to finance your sale at the parameters you've set. Otherwise, you won't be able to realize the $10 million sales price that you were expecting.

Obviously, this, too, requires advance preparation. You can't wait until you're ready to sell your business to find financing sources. These should be developed well ahead of time (you may well need them anyway for other purposes) and nurtured. You can do this through networking, attending civic events, joining chambers of commerce, and asking other business owners.

If you can't find a source to finance the $10 million sale price and your proposed buyer doesn't have $10 million in cash to pay you, then where do you stand? First, you'd better sit!

You must go back to the drawing board and revisit your assumptions. Why are you unable to find the financing for your $10 million sale price? Perhaps your asking price is too high. Or, perhaps there are other factors in play. In any case, putting yourself in your buyer's shoes proves to you why this exercise is valuable in helping you meet your valuation goals.

As a preventive measure, you can have a "trusted other" play the role of the buyer and raise questions, perform due diligence, and tell you they're struggling with financing. Consider this an "exhibition game" before the real season begins. In this way, you can work out the various scenarios which may transpire.

The key is to prevent as many potential problems as you can and to be able to take effective contingent action if prevention fails and the problems arise anyway.

TREAT THE BUSINESS LIKE IT'S FOR SALE EVERY DAY

In order to put yourself in the best position to meet your business sales goal, the most valuable course of action is to treat your business like it's for sale every day. There's an old naval slogan, "If it moves, salute it. If you can't salute it, move it. If you can't move it, paint it."

You need to walk around your business as you would a ship that's dependent on being in top shape despite the rigors of the elements. We tend to allow things to deteriorate not so much out of neglect, but out of misplaced priorities. We'll "get to it when we can," and if we eventually can't, we treat it as a "necessary evil."

People aren't impressed by a messy workplace, whether a personal office or a plant floor or an assortment of cubicles. They don't associate sloppiness with hard work, they associate it with disorganization. That applies to customers, job seekers, *and especially potential buyers for the business.* The way you are organized physically reflects the way you're organized mentally.

If you walk into an auto dealership service facility, you can usually be safe eating off the floor. The places are cleaner than most hospital lobbies. That's because management understands that buyers are leaving their precious possessions there (and, in fact, they often take prospective buyers there to those areas to demonstrate the care taken in all aspects of the business).

When you've been in medical offices with brimming trash receptacles, year-old magazines, and faded health advisories on the wall, what do you think? Probably that no one is really paying attention to the place. And when you see the doctor's desk piled high with bulletins, newsletters, reports, and journals, you have to wonder whether the doctor has been reading them and is up-to-date.

People *do* judge books by their covers and they do make assessments based on the "physical plant." If a realtor takes me to view expensive houses in a ten-year-old (or unwashed or dented) car, I'm not coming back.

FISCAL FINESSE

It may be "homey" and comfortable if you have your dog with you in the office, but not if he pees on the carpets. Or, in the case of President Biden's dogs, if they bite people in the halls.

Build quality relationships with your employees, customers, and vendors that will withstand the ups and downs of the business cycle. One of the great strengths in building a saleable business at any time is a workforce which is stable and excellent. Retention is a key factor. No one wants to buy a business where continual training and retraining are required, both from a time and expense standpoint.

The same applies not only to your customers, of course, but also to your vendors. Don't just pursue cheapest price, develop long-term relationships where you receive high priority and very timely service from suppliers. (Paying your local bills immediately on receipt is a great way to ensure that relationship.) Treat your best customers carefully, not as if everyone is equal.

Create an employee of the week, a benefit for your best suppliers, and/or special customer status for high-end business and long-term loyalty.

Create products and services that meet or exceed your profit margin goals, so that you can build and maintain a strong financial position in your business. This is no time to be conservative. It's time to intelligently invest in products and services that can boost profitability now and in the future.

Football teams have a bad habit of often utilizing a "prevent defense" which is meant to try to protect a lead late in a game. It really becomes a "prevents us from winning" defense, because it sacrifices what has worked for some time in the game and changes everything to ultra-conservatism. In my observation, it adds far more to the probability of losing than of winning. It avoids prudent risk and gives the advantage to the competition.

So while you want to "prevent" a fine salesperson from leaving, or investing in marginally advantageous technology, you do want to invest in hiring a potentially high-performing salesperson and technology that will accelerate customer ordering, for example. (Be careful about the advice of attorneys here, although this might seem contrariant. Attorneys are notoriously conservative, well-mired in "prevent defenses," and will often try to dissuade you from doing anything at all to change the business prior to a sale—even a distant one. You need to ignore that kind of advice.)

Keep looking in the mirror and asking yourself, "What kinds of improvements and modifications would raise the value for me if I were a buyer?" And then get confirmation from trusted sources. (Families also tend to be very conservative.)

Do your best to make use of borrowed money in a judicious manner, because too much debt can hurt your valuation. We've established earlier that there is nothing innately wrong with debt. We routinely use it for mortgages, auto loans, and short-term time-shifting of consumer and business debt. But we have to show that the debt we've incurred and may presently have is being reduced on a regular basis and will not (with certain exceptions, such as a mortgage on the building) continue post-sale.

Credit scores are important for buyers and sellers. You should be able to show a history of paying off debt in the short term—not overdue payments, collection agencies, credit lines or cards being cancelled, and so forth. These days, even the very act of inquiring about a line of credit or a new credit card can adversely affect your credit score. Keep tabs on it.

It's more positive to take debt short-term and pay it off, even if you have to borrow again somewhat later and pay it off again, rather than to carry the debt longer term and try to save money by paying off only minimum amounts.

You also should make sure that there are no lawsuits pending and any that have been settled in the recent past are favorable to you or can be construed that way. Also ensure that any errors or fraud, for example illicit attempts by people to claim workers' compensation, disability, or unemployment benefits, are documented to show you were not culpable and that you responsibly reported the abuses.

The business environment is constantly changing, so don't be afraid to make changes to your exit strategy along the way. Treating your business like it's for sale every day allows you to take a measured approach and avoid rushing to make changes. You create your exit strategy, tweak it along the way, and then execute it successfully.

When this occurs over a reasonable period of time, you have the luxury of making calm decisions and reversing any poor ones. You can prepare for any business environment that happens to exist when you're actually ready to sell. And you can "cement in" the top talent, best practices, reduced indebtedness, and long-term clients.

One final point: Determine if your buyer is looking for a long-term association, either personally running the business or turning it over to family and/or professional management. Or, is this more of a private equity capital acquisition where the buyer is looking to "flip" the business and make a profit in a relatively short time period? I bring this up not only in regard to preparing the business but also in terms of retaining your top talent and best clients.

We have advised "bootstrapping" to start your business, eschewing outside, burdensome financing. We do the same here in urging you to accept leveraged buyouts as noted above, *but not to agree to sell and work under contract to the new owners.*

It's one thing to put your blood, sweat, and tears into your own business, but it's completely another to do so for someone else's business.

10

Creating Legacy

WHOM DO YOU WANT TO BE?

We shouldn't go through life seeking meaning, we should create meaning for ourselves. Our businesses are an extension of that creation.

Let's emphasize a business that had a mission—a *raison d'etre*—that justifies its existence. Famed strategist Peter Drucker remarked that business is not like a tulip or a cheetah, successful by merely perpetuating the species. It's successful when it contributes to the environment, meaning the general environment and community.

The vision of a business is really a metric that can indicate at various points in time if that mission is being met. For example, a mission of creating the best tasting, safest food flavorings in the world might have a vision of people using the firm's name as synonymous with excellence. (We hear today, "Let's Uber to the restaurant.") People might say "We're the Mercedes of photography" (they once said "Cadillac," which shows how these accolades can easily be lost if we don't also focus on the metrics).

Thus, the question isn't so much the hackneyed, "What do you want to be doing next year?" which evokes tasks, methodology, and activity. The question should be, "Whom do you want to be next year?" That's a much tougher question to ask and answer, and most people need time to think about it because they never have before.

Do you want to be someone building a cathedral, or bringing people closer to God? Do you want to be someone designing a room or creating warm and bright space for quality family life? Do you want to be an emergency medical technician (EMT) professional or a lifesaver?

These questions and answers provide meaning, not someone else's, but your own. Your own meaning, your own metrics. Your own mission and your own vision.

DOI: 10.4324/9781032710983-10

If people don't need drills unless they need holes, and if they aren't impressed by a dentist's equipment or staff but rather by their new smile and absence of pain, then why would people be impressed by your business? Is it because your technology is so good that it quickly processes tax information, or is it because you save them tens of thousands in legal tax avoidance?

Here's an exercise: Take a break and then write down *whom* you would like to be next year and/or what image your business should portray to customers and prospects.

_____

_____

What I want the business to be next year

_____

The image I want to portray to customers and prospects

_____

Most people find this difficult, but that's because they're not accustomed to thinking this way. We should be examining not what we do, but what we create.

You don't teach people to play an instrument, you help them fulfill their talent potential. You don't provide accounting services, you provide legal and ethical financial security. You don't sell furniture, you provide comfort and convenience in people's homes. You don't sell cars, you provide lifestyle transportation.

Therapists, attorneys, coaches, and other people in helping professions make less money than they deserve because they charge for their presence (time) not their improvements. They are charging for the present and not the future.

FISCAL FINESSE

Never charge for the past (your credentials) or the present (your presence). Charge for the future (your lasting improvements and contributions).

WHAT IS THE LASTING CONTRIBUTION OF YOUR BUSINESS?

You spent the prime years of your life building a business from the ground up. You survived the ups and downs of the business cycle. For what do you want to be remembered?

Like the valuation of your business, one's "legacy" isn't created on a deathbed or upon retirement. Legacy is built daily. The question is this: Is each new daily "page" blank, a repeat, written by someone else, *or does it show moving forward and your creation of meaning?*

Your business has created products and services for customers, revenue for suppliers, a return on investors' trust in you, a contribution to your community, and jobs for employees. As a result of your success, you have contributed, as well, in civic participation, paying taxes, and using the services of others. This is what Drucker meant by "contributing to the environment."

We'll address the options for your business continuing below, but for now beyond the "Whom do you want to be?" question, ask yourself, "What do you want your business to be?" Your business is either your primary legacy or the force behind your primary legacy (e.g., philanthropy, family, and so forth). How do you want it regarded after you are no longer controlling it?

This "business legacy" is a key part of the valuation of the business, its purchase, and your preparation for its "staging." Whether or not it's your name above the front door, whether it's Adams Family Hardware or Masterful Hardware, there's a great investment that's been made in the name and the business's contribution to those around and within it.

Who does your business continue to help when it's time for you to move on? Will you make a smooth transfer of loyal and important customers to new ownership? Will your family be treated well, whether the new owners are current employees or investors? What about your suppliers who have come to rely on you and who have given you preferential treatment?

And what of the community, where you have been a volunteer, board member, philanthropic, and even an officeholder? What traditions, associations, memberships, and support would you like to see perpetuated? Are there business assets that you should retain or will they all go to the new owners?

A great deal of this depends on who those new buyers are.

WHO INHERITS, BUYS, OR IS GIFTED THE FIRM?

Do you have a succession plan in place? Let's look at your options.

Does your succession plan involve leaving your business to a family member? If so, will this family member inherit the business sight unseen? Or, has this family member worked in the business, earned their stripes, and is now ready to lead the business to new heights?

Are there other family members who may have the wrong expectation, may feel slighted, and may actually contest the sale or the bequest? This occurs frequently, unfortunately, to closely held companies large and small. It's important not only to have a clear desire yourself, but also to make that clear (and especially so to an executor in the event of your death).

These are key considerations for your legacy, because leaving your business to a family member who has no experience in running it *successfully* is a recipe for failure. On the other hand, leaving your business to a family member who knows the business well, *but is not a good leader*, is also a recipe for failure.

If you're seriously considering a family member to assume control of the leadership of the business (investors aside for the moment)—they can be owners but not executives—then consider some precautions.

- They should have been working in the business for at least five years.
- They should be familiar with key customers.
- They should be capable of wearing the many "hats" we've described.
- They should be familiar with key suppliers.
- They should have served in marketing and/or sales.
- They should have financial acumen.
- They should be familiar with your professional support (lawyers, etc.).
- They should get along well with other family members/investors.

They may have developed some of these experiences and expertise working elsewhere, of course, but familiarity with the daily operation of the business is essential. If you have more than one candidate, then these form an ideal litmus test.

FISCAL FINESSE

Throwing a family member who is unprepared into a key role in the business is like throwing that person in front of a car. Even if they survive the impact, there's going to be a bad accident.

Therefore, your designated family member (or members) who will inherit your business should not only know the business inside and out, they also need to be good leaders. Otherwise, your employees may balk at working for your designated family member and leave the business (or, worse, underperform, which may not be realized).

The traits of an outstanding leader include:

- Comfort with ambiguity and the ability to be calm amid turmoil
- Resilience and the ability to "leap forward" from setbacks
- A desire to talk to customers and employees and to listen carefully
- The ability to make tough decisions, including termination
- A sense of humor and perspective at all times
- Prudent risk and willingness to innovate and change
- Ego modification to put the business before personal gain and praise
- Life-long learning
- Flexibility and the ability to change when needed
- A strong command of language and communication skills.

These are obviously often overlapping, so don't be daunted by the variety. You don't want "sufficient" or "adequate" leadership to take over the company, you want *excellent* leadership. (And if that takeover is not in the immediate future, perhaps you should focus on that list for yourself in the interim!)

The same considerations apply for "gifting" the business to someone. In order to ensure that your business can continue to prosper, the giftee should possess the requisite experience, knowledge, and leadership skills necessary to keep your business thriving.

Such a "gift" is most often made to grown children. But remember the old trope that the first generation creates the business, the second expands it, and the third ruins it. This means two things.

- The children who receive the offer should be carefully prepared and their intent and motivation evaluated. It's one thing to say, "Sure, I'll run the business," and another to be prepared to do so.
- It's quite reasonable to prepare grandchildren to take part in the business when there is still the opportunity to learn from you, the founder, and not only secondhand from their parents. There are cases of this "gifting" passing over one generation and involving the next.

Do you plan to sell your business? If so, the concepts of maximizing valuation covered in Chapter 9 should be part of your prime directive. You'll want to figure out who's in the universe of potential buyers for your business and will they find your valuation reasonable or not.

Just as you seek "ideal customers," you should seek "ideal buyers." This identical concept, illustrated in Chapter 4, is again depicted in Figure 10.1.

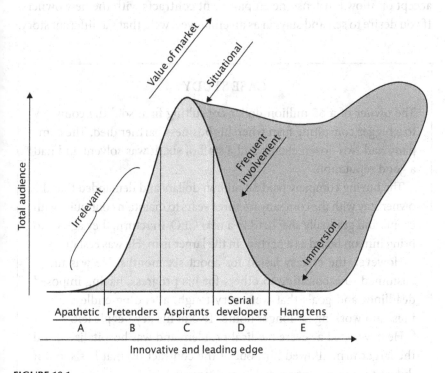

FIGURE 10.1
Finding the ideal buyer. Blog Post by Alan Weiss, "Business of Consulting," November 18, 2011, alanweiss.com, reprinted with permission.

In this standard bell curve, it's not the width that is important but the vertical category and its depth. Toward the middle and left are non-ideal buyers (and/or customers, for that matter). But as you move toward the right, you have a smaller slice but of more high potential buyers. ("Hang ten" is a surfing term denoting those who are willing to take intelligent risks and make innovations in order to improve the ride.)

Thus, you're better off "courting" and evaluating a score or more of buyers on the right than thousands on the left or hundreds in the middle. The key is not in maximizing the quantity of prospects, *but rather in maximizing the quality of the prospects*. That's why the point is that this applies to customers for your business (see Chapter 4), as well as buyers of your business. This will greatly enhance your options to sell, but it's apparent that this search for fewer and better buyers might take quite some time.

Hence, our focus is on long-term preparation and patience.

If you decide to sell your business and really intend on retiring, don't accept or allow burdensome employment contracts with the new owners. If you desire to sell and stay on as an employee, well, that's a different story.

CASE STUDY

The owner of a $5 million dollar consulting firm sold the company to a bigger consulting firm when his business partner died. The company had two dozen clients and a staff of six. It was solvent and had a good reputation.

The buying company paid $8 million dollars and demanded that the owner stay with the company for three years to maintain continuity with clients and gradually shepherd in a new CEO. In return, they agreed to bring him on board as a partner in the larger firm. He was ecstatic.

However, the ecstasy lasted for about six months. He was unaccustomed to accounting to others for his progress, having imposed deadlines and goals that were very tough, attending endless meetings, and working far longer hours. Two of his key people left.

He developed a severe medical problem and was hospitalized, and the larger firm allowed him out of the contract on that basis, but it did cost him some promised bonus money.

Don't think an offer to work for someone else for a few years is a good way to get a quick deal. Instead, it could be a long tribulation.

RETIREMENT ISN'T WHAT YOU THINK IT IS

Have you thought of what retirement would mean for you? For some business owners, retirement is long, sunny days at the beach house with cocktails in hand. For others, there are only so many fish one can catch or hours spent in the hammock.

Retirement became a major issue post-World War II, when Franklin Delano Roosevelt's legislation about Social Security and a "safety net" took hold. But what most people don't realize is that the "safety net" was supposed to include corporate pensions and retirement funds, the extended family that was so common then as a support network, and charities. *Social Security was never meant to subsidize one's life without other forms of income to augment it.*

Moreover, in 1945, there were about 40 people working and depositing into the system for every retired person withdrawing from it, and retirement at 65 resulted in a brief life thereafter—the average lifespan at the time was 68. *Today, there are 2.5 people working for every retired person, and the average lifespan is 78.* Do the math. The system can't survive based on these numbers.

Additionally, morbidity today is higher than fertility, so fewer and fewer people will be entering the workforce (and in large companies, they may be replaced by technology and automation, which pays nothing into Social Security coffers). There are no large extended families providing support anymore (we've often moved far from home and loved ones), and there aren't many other sources for the "safety net."

In fact, the maximum monthly payment today for the very highest contributors waiting the longest time to withdraw (at this writing, 72.5 years) is about $4,500, before various deductions such as Medicare. But even the gross amount of $54,000 annually isn't going to provide for a very comfortable retirement unless you have private savings and investments, and a business that will be highly valuable when you're ready to sell it.

During my career, I have observed entrepreneurs with vastly different personality types. The common denominator that these different personality types possess is that they don't want to completely stop working. They constantly need to be busy doing "something."

So "retirement" isn't really a new life of sitting back watching TV, tending a garden, and playing with the grandchildren (or the dog). It's a time of less pressure, but not necessarily less contribution.

FISCAL FINESSE

With the nation suffering a loss of labor because the population is no longer replacing itself, accessing the wisdom of people who started and successfully ran their own businesses will be critical for the profit, non-profit, and governmental sectors. "Wisdom" is generally not found in 25-year-olds.

This dynamic also applies to academia, where remote learning is going to take on more and more of a significant role, and "retired" resources can be important faculty contributors. Don't be loath to give up running your business because you feel it's somehow "the end." *It simply marks a new beginning.*

Based on my experience, I am convinced that the entrepreneurial personality type doesn't have a "switch" that they can simply turn off. They are born with a certain fire in their belly. They can't just "stop."

That means the potential sale of your business may be to another entrepreneur who wants to "get back in the game." And *that* means that it's wise to develop relationships with these people throughout your career. When someone else "retires" or sells their business to pursue other interests, don't drop them as if they've left your club. Remain in touch because they or someone they know may turn out to be your eventual buyer.

The ways you develop these contacts and participate in such communities of owners may be through the chamber of commerce, Rotary, veterans associations, civic volunteer groups, by serving on nonprofit boards, donating to charities and participating in their events, and so forth.

There are also mastermind groups, some casually formed, some hosted by third parties for a fee, in which you'll meet kindred spirits and others who are looking to enlarge and/or add to their own business holdings. These are sources of continuing education for you, helpful comparisons on your own progress, and highly valuable resources as you make plans to improve your valuation and eventually sell your business.

You don't really ever "retire" from entrepreneurialism!

How many times have you heard stories about entrepreneurs coming out of retirement for another try at entrepreneurship? Not all are successful. The major difference seems to be their understanding and implementation of sound business practices. Note that here I didn't say "familiarity with the business." A great many people have sold their businesses, become bored, and tried their hand at running another business.

But the fallacy is that they believe if it's the same business—hardware, accounting, auto sales, signage, furniture, or whatever—as their prior one, they'll be naturally good, just by "picking up where they left off." But it's not *content* knowledge that makes the difference, it's *process* knowledge.

In other words, you need to know how to run a business, because the principles are the same even if the products and services are different. That's why you see prior, successful business owners fail when they buy the same type of business as their previous one, and others succeed in even radically different businesses than their previous one.

If you're skeptical about this, consider that IBM was "saved" when it was in horrible shape by Lou Gerstner, who came from RJR Nabisco, a food company! A lot of people were horrified until he restored IBM to a world-class operation. The converse is Jeff Immelt, the long-time GE executive who knew the company very well and succeeded Jack Welch when he retired. From that day to this, GE has fallen out of the lists of the world's best companies and has been divided into three companies with over $60 billion in debt and its stock has fallen by over 80 percent.

It's the *process* of how to run a business that's crucial, in any size operation, and not merely *content* knowledge. Just ask GE shareholders.

This discussion is obviously aimed at the future, "post-retirement." It's not too soon to consider that, either!

I know that I can't retire because I don't want to. My hope is that I can remain healthy enough to be able to continue to work as a business consultant because I absolutely love my work. Maybe my work will become part-time work. Who knows? I don't know what the future holds, but I know that I don't want to sit on a beach full-time, all the time. I need to be continuously tinkering with something in order to maintain a sense of satisfaction and accomplishment.

There is an abundance of ways we can contribute to our family, community, and society in general. As successful business owners, we're valuable and capable of helping others in a variety of formal and informal manners. The point is that the time to start thinking about all of this is *now*. That's why we're ending with these thoughts, so that you can immediately put the book down and begin considering what actions to take. You want to make decisions from a position of strength.

Can you relate to what I'm describing? If so, picture in your mind what "retirement" scenario would work for you and make it a reality!

Index

Pages in *italics* refer to figures and pages followed by "n" refer to notes